D1549392

WALKING THE SCOTTISH BORDER

Walking
The Scottish Border

BOB LANGLEY

ROBERT HALE · LONDON

© Robert Langley 1976
First published in Great Britain 1976
Reprinted 1976

ISBN 0 7091 5300 7

Robert Hale Limited
Clerkenwell House
Clerkenwell Green
London EC1R OHT

Filmset by Specialised Offset Services Ltd., Liverpool
and printed in Great Britain by
Redwood Burn Limited
Trowbridge & London

Contents

Illustrations

Preface

This book is the direct result of a television film in which I hiked along the Scottish Border from the Solway Firth to the North Sea. When the series first appeared on BBC's 'Pebble Mill' programme (and later under the seperate title of 'The Border Line') letters poured in from people who wanted to do the walk for themselves. It is in response to those letters, and in particular to their requests for hints and suggestions that I have jotted down my impressions and experiences. It is not meant to be a definitive work on the Border by any means. It is simply the record of a journey along its length as it seemed to me at the time. The adventures were personal adventures, and the reactions and sensations were personal too. I realize I was in a privileged position: as a television reporter, I did the hike as part of my job and got paid for doing it, but I enjoyed the experience immensely, and I hope this book will prompt others to try it too. I believe that, at the very least, it will give them a fair picture of what to expect on the way.

Apart from a couple of instances, I have veered off the actual filming because I feel that is a separate story. I would however, like to take this opportunity to thank my director Matthew Robinson for his boundless enthusiasm and patience, and my film crew who inevitably display all the guts and enjoy little of the glory. I am also indebted to my producers Terry Dobson and Roger Laughton, and to my boss Phil Sidey who started the thing rolling in the first place.

The Border verses I have quoted in various places in this account are all from *2000 Miles of Wandering in the Border Country* by Edward Bogg of Leeds, published jointly by him and John Sampson of York in 1898.

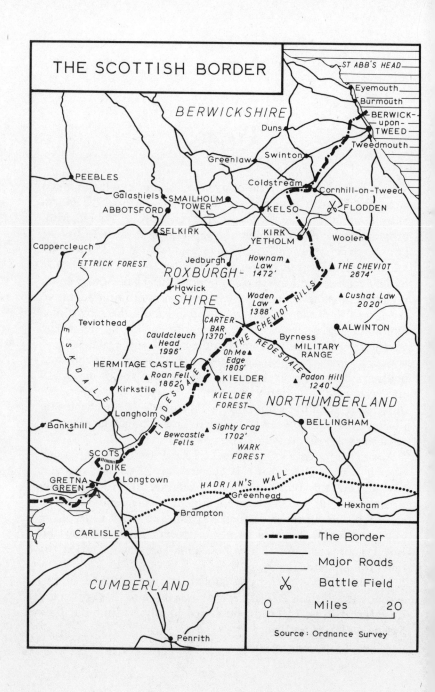

THE SCOTTISH BORDER

ST ABB'S HEAD

BERWICKSHIRE

Eyemouth
Burmouth
BERWICK-upon-TWEED
Tweedmouth
Duns
Greenlaw
Swinton
Coldstream
Cornhill-on-Tweed
PEEBLES
Galashiels
SMAILHOLM TOWER
ABBOTSFORD
KELSO
FLODDEN
SELKIRK
KIRK YETHOLM
Wooler
Cappercleuch
ETTRICK FOREST
Jedburgh
Hownam Law 1472'
▲ THE CHEVIOT 2674'
ROXBURGH-SHIRE
Hawick
Woden Law 1388'
▲ *Cushat Law 2020'*
Teviothead
CARTER BAR 1370'
THE CHEVIOT HILLS
ALWINTON
Cauldcleuch Head 1996'
THE REDESDALE
Byrness
MILITARY RANGE
Oh Me Edge 1809'
HERMITAGE CASTLE
▲ *Roan Fell 1862'*
KIELDER
▲ *Padon Hill 1240'*
Kirkstile
LIDDESDALE
KIELDER FOREST
NORTHUMBERLAND
Langholm
BELLINGHAM
Bankshill
Sighty Crag 1702'
Bewcastle Fells
WARK FOREST
SCOTS DIKE
GRETNA GREEN
Longtown
HADRIAN'S WALL
Greenhead
Hexham
Brampton
CARLISLE

CUMBERLAND

Penrith

━·━·━ The Border

────── Major Roads

✂ Battle Field

0 — Miles — 20

Source: Ordnance Survey

1

Raiders' Path

The train stopped. A hollow tannoyed voice said: "This is Carlisle, this is Carlisle," and I woke up.

A negro porter clattered by the window on a mobile parcel truck. There was a smell of diesel fumes mingled with hot coffee from the nearby refreshment stall. The air felt damp and heavy with a faint chill to remind me that I had just travelled several hundred miles north.

I grabbed my haversack from the luggage rack and shuffled on to the platform, through the ticket barrier and out to the taxi rank and car park.

It was Saturday night and the pubs were out. Drunken singing echoed between the shiny fronts of modern department stores. Cars hissed by, their tyres making a sucking noise on the gleaming asphalt. Mist hung like streamers between the streetlamps. This was Carlisle, Gateway to the Border, and, it had seemed to me, the ideal jumping off spot to begin my journey. At that moment it seemed like the last place on earth. Eleven o'clock on a Saturday night is a bad time for first impressions. Sober ones, that is.

When I got to the hotel, the night porter was on duty. I had to ring four times before he appeared, a small balding man with a purple razor-scraped jaw and bushy eyebrows which curled into points like the feelers on a beetle.

"I phoned earlier to say I'd be late," I said, "My name is Langley."

He ran his finger down the register.

"Ah yes, Mr Langley, if you'd just sign here please."

The heavy eyebrows drew together as he peered at my haversack and boots. I watched his eyes dance over me from head to toe. He looked puzzled.

"Going on a trip?" he murmured conversationally.

"I'm walking the Scottish Border," I said.

The heavy eyebrows lifted.

"All of it?"

"Yes."

"Why that's ... that's. ..."

"One hundred and ten miles," I prompted.

He fumbled among the rows of room keys, giving me the kind of sidelong glance one usually reserves for lunatics.

"Doing it for fun, are you?" he muttered, picking up my haversack.

I thought for a moment.

"No," I said, "Wages."

"Ah," he said with relief, as if the mention of money brought the venture back into the realms of sanity, "Wages, is it? Very nice, very nice indeed. I wish someone would pay me wages to do a thing like that. The Scottish Border. Well now, there's a beautiful bit of country and no mistake. This way, Mr Langley."

We walked along corridors where the carpet was worn to a frazzle like moulding lace. There was the pungent scent of disinfectant mingled with the smell of cigarette smoke and stale breath.

"Carlisle man yourself, are you?" I inquired gently.

The razor-scraped jaw split into a broad grin.

"Born and bred," he said with pride.

"I suppose you'll know all about the Border then?"

He frowned.

"Well, to tell the truth," he said, "It's a bit out of the way, isn't it."

"It's only a few miles north," I said.

"I mean it's a bit difficult to get to. It's not the sort of place you can drive along in a car."

"But if you've lived in Carlisle all your life, the Border must be in your blood. The old moss troopers," I prompted, "the raiders, the reivers, the Border ballads, that sort of thing."

He stared at me mildly.

"Mr Langley," he said, "that was a long time ago. It's not like that now."

He paused to unlock my door, then stepped back to let me

through. The room was small and compact. Cooking fumes drifted through the open window. I could see the shiny rooftiles of the houses across the street.

I tipped him and he smiled pleasantly.

"Can I have a call at six-thirty?" I asked.

"That's a bit early for breakfast," he said, "The chef doesn't come on till seven. But I'll try and get you some toast."

At the door, he paused.

"About the Border," he muttered, "It's just that ... well, we're the same country these days, aren't we, we're all under the same queen? It's not like a real border any more."

"No," I said understandingly, "Not a real border."

He smiled again.

"Goodnight," I said, "And thankyou."

After he had gone, I stood at the window and smoked a small cheroot. Across the rooftops, I could see the darkened hump of red sandstone that was Carlisle Castle, site of the ancient roman town of Luguvallium. My first Border stronghold. I peered at it through the gloom with a strange fascination. The sky behind the turrets looked mottled and angry, touched with red from the city streetlamps like the hammered bottom of a copper pot. It was a sky to steer away from, to button up against, a cloud-hung, wind-blown, rain-spattered sky. I shuddered. Tomorrow, and for the next few days, rain or wind, sleet or shine, my only shelter would be the tiny pup tent in the haversack on my back as I followed the trail of the Border Line across 110 miles of some of the wildest and most spectacular scenery in.Britain. It would not be an easy walk, I knew that. There were few paths, and even fewer areas of habitation. Directly in my way stood the Border Forest, the largest man-made forest in Europe. Beyond it stretched the open freeway of the Cheviot Hills, flanked by the military ranges of Redesdale and Otterburn.

Unlike Offa's Dyke or the Pennine Way, the Scottish Border was not a national footpath, and because of the scarcity of highways had managed to remain largely intact, unspoiled by the incursion of the main summer tourist routes. It was, I knew, a unique region – once the most disputed territory in the country. A land of wild hills, ancient castles and famous abbeys which had seen more turbulence and more bloodshed than the rest of these

islands put together. I would be following in the footsteps of the
old moss troopers, those outlaws of ancient times who spread
terror and devastation along the Border counties, for this was
once Britain's wild west, North West Frontier, Berlin Wall, call
it what you will: a place where blackmail, rape, looting, arson,
kidnapping and wholesale murder were considered an essential
part of the social graces, and where the Border Line itself was
conceived in more than a thousand years of the bloodiest battles
in our history.

I peered silently at the huddled outline of Carlisle Castle.
Beneath the neon-splashed sky it looked oddly out of place, and
yet Carlisle Castle caught the very essence of the Border. It was
some fortress, that one: a symbol of austerity no doubt, for the
prisoners of the Wars of the Roses who were confined there, and
for Mary, Queen of Scots who took refuge in its fourteenth-
century tower after her escape from Lochleven Castle. It had
withstood siege for nine months against Parliamentary forces
during the Civil War, and had entertained Bonnie Prince
Charlie and his 'hundred pipers' in 1745. (It entertained several of
his leaders again after the quenching of the Jacobite rebellion,
when their heads were set on spikes along the city walls.) It was
also the scene of one of the earliest commando raids when, on the
night of 13th April 1596, the bold Buccleuch crossed the Esk
with eighty men and pounded on the castle gates, demanding the
release of Kinmont Willie – an attack which, by its very daring,
caused Queen Elizabeth to exclaim: "With ten thousand such
men, our cousin the King of Scotland might shake the firmest
throne in Europe".

Stirring stuff: but that is what the Border was all about – gory
deeds, fierce loyalties and even fiercer treachories. For the next
few days I would be stepping back into its past, tracing its
wriggling diversions and deviations, and recapturing some of the
colour and tradition that made it such a romantic and fascinating
locality.

I turned and peered at my hotel bed. It looked snugly inviting,
the starched sheets turned primly down, the pillows puffed
prettily up. Might as well make the most of it, I thought. I
stubbed out my cheroot, took off my clothes and switched off the
light.

9th June, 8.30 a.m. The sky looked bleak and menacing as I set off along the rim of the Solway Firth. Over west, a few pastel-tipped clouds scurried eastward, turning the flat sheen of the Sark Estuary into the colour of Burgundy wine. I recalled the old proverb: 'a red sky in the morning,' and sniffed the air. Rain later, I thought, and as if on cue a few drops pattered against my skin. An early-morning fisherman in thigh-length waders grinned at me from the shallows.

"Nasty day," I remarked.

He chuckled.

"Aye, the weather's just broken," he said, "You should have been here yesterday."

That is what people always say. You should have been here yesterday. Half my life is spent in places I should have been in yesterday.

I pulled out my parka, tugged it on, and set off along the bank of the river Sark, the rain and wind-whipped sea-spray biting at my cheeks. Behind me, far across the Solway, high mountains leaned dourly into a swirling sky. Ahead, the river weaved its way through green fields and rainsoaked meadows where clumps of marsh grass clogged my path and cattle huddled mournfully under soggy hedgerows.

As the rain trickled down my hair and gathered in great globules on my ear lobes, I thought with some nostalgia of my warm hotel bed and wondered what had happened to the Border I had geared myself to expect, the Border of colour and romance? The only colours I could see were the far-off silvery glimpses of the Solway, and the rolling masses of dark blue cloud surging in from the west. And who could think of romance with trousers plastered soggily from ankle to hip? After less than an hour, the whole venture was rapidly souring in my mind, and I still had 110 miles to go.

Now 110 miles may not sound a very great distance, but there is a world of difference between walking 110 miles along a level paved highway, and slogging 110 miles over trackless hill and moorland. If anyone is planning to try it for himself, let me underline that point with some emphasis: it is best to know what you are letting yourself in for. If you do not like getting wet, or chilled, or if the prospect of struggling to heat a can of beans in a force eight gale does not appeal to you, settle down in front of the fireplace and read a good book: I am a dedicated armchair adventurer myself. If, on the other hand, you decide after the next few chapters that the Border is a 'must' for next summer, let me give you a useful rundown on the contents of my rucksack.

Mountaineering has been a hobby of mine for years, but I must confess that in spite of repeated warnings in the newspapers and on TV, I have always been lackadaisical about equipment. I remember when I did the Pennine Way for BBC Television, several people wrote to complain that I was wearing jeans. Jeans, they said, should not be worn in the great outdoors, for they could get wet and result in the wearer suffering from exposure. Well, this may be so, but I have worn jeans in the Canadian Rockies, the Swiss Alps, the Pyrenees, the Sierra Madre, and the British Columbia Coastal Range. I have worn them in desert heat, in biting cold, in blizzards and torrential rain, and they have never let me down yet. But if you prefer to play it absolutely safe, then I suppose flannel, woollen or cord trousers are best. Keep off corduroys which tend to take a long time to dry out. On good days you may decide to wear shorts, but make sure you have got a good pair of over-trousers handy in case the weather changes. The important thing is to have protection from the wind. A strong gale can squeeze out your energy – and your body heat – faster than anything going, and when you come up against a gale coupled with freezing rain or sleet, then you really are into exposure conditions.

As far as anoraks go, buy one that is suitably windproof, with a hood, long sleeves and enough material below to cover your bottom and lower abdomen. I would like to say get one that is waterproof as well, but rubberised materials 'sweat' a lot once you start moving, and you can end up as damp from condensation as you can from a steady downpour.

If you are doing the Border in winter, you will need a good pair of gloves. Most people find that mitts with one basic compartment for the four main fingers are warmer than the ordinary fivepronged ones. Make sure they have got long wrists and that, like your trousers and anorak, they are windproof. It might be a good idea too in winter, to wear some kind of headgear. You will have your anorak hood of course, but a little woollen cap, or better still, a balaclava helmet which covers the ears and throat would be a worthwhile investment. In any event, winter is not the best time for walking the Border. Far better wait for summer or spring, not just for safety's sake, but also because there is so much more to enjoy. Winter or summer though, I think the main thing is to keep warm and relatively dry. But above all – and this is terribly important – travel light. An overweight rucksack can grind you into the ground in really rough country. On one trip down the Pennine range, I had to jettison nearly thirty per cent of my equipment, including a stove, spare gas cylinders, pots and pans, dress shoes and plimsolls.

Using a bit of thought when packing your rucksack can make a tremendous difference too. Try and keep the weight as high as possible and directly over the spine. Far better to have it pressing down on your back than dangling from your shoulders. Choose a pack frame or a V-shape rucksack and make sure that the load is well balanced. A pack that is heavier on one side than the other can throw you over. Make allowances for your rucksack's weight when you are walking, particularly coming downhill. And it is worth getting your hands on a large polythene bag to use as an inner waterproof lining.

If I did it again, I think perhaps I would camp out less. A tent is a handy thing to have along: it gives you a certain independence and it makes a useful shelter if you run into trouble, but apart from crossing the Cheviots I could have reached the odd guest house or hotel here and there if I had put my mind to it. I mention this in case there are would-be walkers who are put off by the prospect of spending a week or so out in the open. As long as you are prepared to rough it for at least one night between Carter Bar and Kirk Yetholm then you should be able to muck through by making the occasional detour to look for accommodation. Remember that although there are no hotels at Kielder, there is a youth hostel, and a few miles up the Newcastleton road you will find a farmhouse offering bed and breakfast. Nevertheless, always be prepared for the worst: you never know when you are likely to be benighted, and if the idea of hauling a tent around does not appeal to you, at least make sure you have got some sort of sleeping bag, with a plastic survival sack.

Food will naturally be one of your major considerations. You have got to eat, after all: and yet, a loaf of bread and a few cans of this and that can take up an enormous amount of precious rucksack room. In most camping shops you can buy concentrated foods designed for high-altitude climbers. These are little packets of powder which, mixed with water, turn into a reasonable facsimile of curries, stews and the like. Personally, I think they are a bad buy. By all means include a packet or two in case of emergency, but after spending the day slogging through wild hills, the one thing you need at the end of it is something suitably mouth-watering, and mouth-watering iron rations I am afraid have yet to be invented. I was interested to hear from Chris Bonington that British Himalayan expeditions are beginning to veer away from concentrated foods, and are taking with them supplies of tinned paté, salami, tinned Dundee cake and other luxuries which give a whole new meaning to the idea of 'roughing it'. So take what you find tastiest, bearing in mind of course that it will get some rough handling on the way. (Remember eggs crack, tomatoes squash.) Tinned foods are best: not too many tins, mind you, for they will drag down your rucksack like nobody's business – just enough to get you through to the next village. There are plenty of places en route to replenish supplies: it is just a question of plotting out the sections where you are likely to run into trouble. You will need to stock up before crossing the Cheviot Hills for instance, and possibly before entering the Border Forest, but as a general rule, getting food on the Border is not a major problem.

If you intend to stay at boarding houses for most of the way I would say that the best plan would be to stick to cold stuff. If you can pick up a packed lunch and say a thermos flask of hot coffee at each stopping point, you will be cutting down a lot on storage space and weight. Staying in hotels or guest houses also gives you the marvellous luxury of a properly-cooked meal each evening, and for the odd night you *have* to spend in the open, you can always put up with cold cheese butties or something, knowing you will be back to the smoked salmon and Chateaubriand in twenty-four hours.

If, on the other hand, you are determined to cook, then better carry a little something in reserve – a pocketful of cold rations – just in case torrential rains put out your fire. Cheese is a good bet. Salmon or sardines. And an apple or two. There is no gloomier

sensation in the world than sitting in a soggy wood eating cold
beans out of the tin, with water dripping off the end of your
nose. Do not be tempted into carrying a stove. It is just not worth
it from the weight point of view. And a last reminder about
lighting fires: please be careful – keep well away from
woodland, and do make sure the fire is well and truly out before
you move on.

The one piece of equipment you cannot do without is a good
reliable compass. A compass is as essential to a venture like this as
is a strong pair of legs. Without it, you simply would not come
out at the other end. You also need a full set of Ordnance Survey
maps, one-inch-to-the-mile: there are four in all covering the
Border. Know how to read those maps, know how to use that
compass: those are the first and most important steps and I cannot
stress them too strongly. It is a good idea to study the maps
beforehand, so that you have a good mental image of your route,
with valleys, hills and ridges clearly set out in your mind. This
gives you a certain advantage if you get trapped by mist, a
common occurrence on the Border. The Border hills are small
and easily under-estimated: just remember that the sea is never
more than thirty-five miles away, and with the sea that close, the
weather is bound to be unpredictable. I always think it is better
to look on the black side: expect the worst and prepare for it.

Since my BBC walk programmes, I have received a good
many letters from people about to tackle long-distance hikes, and
I have often been amazed at how little some of them know about
just what to expect. One woman wrote to me asking if the
Scottish Border would make a pleasant mid-winter stroll for the
children (aged eight to eleven). Another wanted to know if she
would need a map, or would the route be clearly signposted? A
man in Lewes asked if the Pennine Way was gentle enough for
someone with a severe heart condition? So at the risk of repeating
myself, let me say once more and as strongly as I can: the Scottish
Border may be only 110 miles long, but you really can land
yourself in trouble if you tackle it without being properly
prepared. Mind you, do not go mad and buy up the entire
contents of the Army and Navy Store. Common sense is the
keyword: keep warm, keep dry – know where to go and how to
get there.

Inside my pack I carried a waterproof suit (which also served as a groundsheet by night), a spare shirt, socks and underclothing, one spare sweater, a metal mug-cum-pot which could be used either for drinking or for boiling water to brew tea, a sleeping bag and a tiny one-man pup tent. Unfortunately, the pup tent when erected was only six feet long, which meant that my feet stuck out the bottom, but it had served me well during a three year trip around North America and its overall weight, neatly-rolled, was less than three pounds. The socks were thick and woolly, for my experience has been that once socks get really sweaty, the friction of movement tends to rub at the skin itself, and chafed ankles in the middle of the Cheviot Hills can turn an enjoyable walk into a gruelling endurance test. Lastly, I wore a good strong pair of boots. Opinions seem to differ as far as footwear is concerned. For long-range walking, some people prefer the lightweight kind, with pliable uppers and moulded-rubber soles. Others rely on the good old army variety with heavy metal studs. Personally, I have always gone for the less expensive form of climbing boot, one which has both an inner and outer casing so that the ankle is firmly supported. It does tend to get over-heavy when clogged with mud, but at least there is no danger of the boot coming to pieces in rough terrain. Commando soles are a great advantage over the old-fashioned metal studs. The rubber can prove slippery when wet, but in the long run it cushions the bottom of the feet against continual slithering and scrabbling.

You can, if you wish, include a torch and a whistle: I know the rule book says you should, but if you follow the rule book word for word you will probably never get beyond your garden gate. I remember once interviewing a world-famous mountaineer about safety in the hills, and after advising would-be ramblers to carry rescue blankets, padded overjackets and everything, in fact, but the kitchen sink, he added rather lamely, "Of course I never do myself".

Use your head: if it is summer-time in Britain, the worst you can expect on the Border are heavy winds and non-stop rain, but remember too that once on that ridge, there is no place to shelter – you will have to see it through to the bitter end.

Thinking about time, I would say a fair estimate for someone who is fit would be five to six days, but it seems a shame to turn the walk into a race – you miss so much that way. A full week would give you a better margin. If you can manage ten days or a fortnight, that would be better still – you would have lots of time to play around with then, so you could make the odd trip to places of interest and still have a few days in hand in case things go wrong.

If you are one of those people who likes to plan out the route day by day, be sure to make allowances for rough country. You may be able to walk twenty or thirty miles along a smooth tarmac road, but you would need to be in remarkably good shape to do that in the Cheviot Hills. Do not attempt to cover the same distance every day. Take the nature of the land into account. You may go like the clappers in the flat country between the Solway and Gretna Green, but you are bound to slow down when you reach the fringes of the Border Forest. Apart from the Forestry roads, the ground between Hobb's Flow and Carter Bar is very lumpy and boggy and could hold you up considerably. Remember too that after two or three days your muscles may well be stiff and sore and you will not be in the mood for pushing yourself to the limit. Daily distances will vary according to individual strengths and abilities, but the beauty of the Border walk is that so long as you give yourself enough time, you can do it at your own pace.

If you intend to visit historical monuments, then these too must be taken into account. The best jumping-off point for Hermitage Castle for instance, is to follow the old coal road from Bloody Bush, but take note that this will add at least six and a half miles to your journey. Trying to reach Hermitage from Carter Bar, as I did, is a rather silly move because by then you are doubling back on your tracks and the only sensible thing is to hitch-hike. I do not think it is cheating to thumb the odd lift between Coldstream and Smailholm Tower say, or to pick up a bus as far as Kelso. You are making a detour after all, it is not as if you are chickening out on the actual hike.

One other thing: if you are intent on going it alone, then be prepared for a lonely time. I know this seems an obvious statement, but it is amazing just how lonely you can feel after only a couple of days without seeing anybody. The hills can be awfully oppressive if you are not used to long silences. The days are long, and there are no recreational outlets for the evenings. If the weather is bad then you are stuck with that too. In other words, the enjoyment lies in the isolation and solitude, so if you do decide to do it solo, then make sure in your own mind that you are the kind of person who really does enjoy his own company. To anyone who is the least bit gregarious I would say: take a companion along. You will enjoy it all the more, and it is safer with two or more people anyhow.

As I sloshed along the muddy bank of the river Sark, the spray lashing into my face, I thought wistfully that being a TV reporter sounds a lot more romantic than it actually is. People often say, "It must be an interesting life you lead". I know it *sounds* interesting. It even sounds interesting to *me*. But largely it is a hotch-potch of cold hotel rooms, draughty train corridors and endless boring hours of just hanging about. All interspersed with episodes of extreme physical discomfort. At that moment I wished with all my heart that I worked in a bank. Or a garage. Or a toolshop. Or that I had been a nightwatchman, sitting in his snug little brazier-warmed hut.

I leaned heavily into the wind as a swirl of gulls rose yelping above my head, sweeping westward across the Solway. Boulders nudged through the grass, gleaming wetly like half-submerged turnips. The Firth was a blur of silvery-white, merging almost imperceptibly with a steel-grey sky. It is a strange place in many ways, the Solway Firth, not really like the sea at all, but more like a gap between two great land masses, as if everything has somehow been mixed up together, mountains, pastures, and ocean, to form a spectacular and wildly intricate prototype for geology students. The interesting thing is that over the centuries the Solway has been steadily receding. One tends to think of the sea as an erosive agent, nibbling away at the land like an enormous cuckoo taking bigger and bigger bites. But the Solway is just the opposite. Areas which are now rich farm soil were once covered by the in-coming tide, so the sea is actually receding. Inch by inch, foot by foot, it is falling back, leaving a steadily-increasing section of countryside ready to be ploughed up and harvested.

On the night of 17th November, 1771, the dark oily peat

which lies hidden below the sands and which had been force-fed by several weeks of torrential rain, suddenly swelled up and burst through the surface like a monster emerging from the bowels of the earth. Lava-like, the peat oozed its way over hundreds of acres of countryside, smothering cattle, burying farms, forcing the inhabitants to flee through the darkness, leaving their livestock and possessions to be engulfed by the creeping suffocating wall. It was an extraordinary tragedy, totally unexpected and unprecedented, and I am happy to say that there has been no repetition of it since, but as the rain came pitter-pattering down my cheeks, I could not help putting on an instinctive spurt.

In the meadows, the cows looked drenched and sombre. Farmhouses peeked through drip-dreary trees. For the next few miles, I knew, my path would be devious and uneventful, tracing all the twists and turns of the river. But although the Border *follows* natural lines, it is never a natural line in itself. It took centuries of bitter fighting to establish, and even when it *was* established, it kept changing with the fortunes of war.

It was the Romans who started it all back in A.D. 122 when they built Hadrian's Wall. This huge rampart, dotted with watch-towers and fortified villages ran from Bowness-on-Solway to Wallsend-on-Tyne, slicing across the narrowest neck of Britain and dividing for the first time, the countries to the north and south. That was its primary purpose – not merely to keep the barbarians in the north in check, as is commonly supposed (the wall in those days was easily overrun) but to be a kind of dividing line.

The way the Wall came about is interesting in itself. For a long time, the Romans had been casting their eyes northward toward Scotland. Mind you, they had done a damn good job of parcelling up the Border country as it was: the governor, Iulius Agricola had carved it into an effective military web of garrison forts and roads. Some of that web still exists: Dere Street for example, which formed the main route north from York to the Firth and which is considered today to be a brilliant piece of engineering, still slices its way boldly across the Cheviot Hills. With this road-and-fortress network, Agricola was able to cordon off the native communities and bring a certain level of law and order to what was, by its very nature, a lawless country. At Corbridge-on-Tyne he stationed the largest cavalry regiment in the north – one thousand strong. At High Rochester, he maintained a second regiment, 500 strong, made up partly of cavalry, partly of infantry. Another 500 dragoons waited at Learchild and between them they levied what must seem today a rough-and-ready brand of justice, wholly one-sided, but bringing at least a blueprint for guaranteed peace.

In A.D. 79, Agricola began to push north, and five years later had thrust the boundaries of the Roman Empire to the very foothills of the Highlands. Not for long however, for military outposts proved extremely difficult to maintain in such mountainous country. By A.D. 105, all the territory north of the Cheviots had to be abandoned, and the Emperor Hadrian decided to draw a line across the slender throat of Britain, the firmest line still held by Roman garrisons, and mark once and for all the end of the civilized world as the Romans saw it, and the start of the wilderness.

The wall took five years in all to build, which seems a remarkable achievement even in this day and age: but then, apart from the three legions who actually laid and constructed it, the Romans used largely slave labour for the heavy work. At the end of that time, they had one of the most remarkable barricades in history, seventy miles long, twenty feet high, ten feet wide, and sustained by intervening fortresses and a great boundary ditch known as the Vallum. There has been a good deal of speculation about the Vallum, for it is not clear precisely what its purpose was. After all, the wall presents a defensive line facing north: the existence of a further barrier on the southern side – the side which should by rights be Roman-controlled, is a little confusing. The most popular theory is that the building of the wall aroused a good deal of hostility among neighbouring tribes, and that the second barrier was built to prevent Roman patrols being taken from the rear by angry locals.

The nature of the wall changed drastically throughout the years of the Roman occupation. It had originally been intended to have the garrison forts at some distance behind it, but this was later altered to absorb the forts into the barrier itself. Some decades later, when a new wall was constructed between the Forth and Clyde, the patrolling system on Hadrian's Wall was temporarily abandoned and the doors removed from the milecastle gateways. By A.D. 158 however, when the whole area had broken into violent revolt, Hadrian's Wall was re-occupied and its castles and turrets brought into use once again.

This then was the first border, the first attempt to draw a line across the country and divide it into two. But it was long after the Romans had gone that the real turmoil began. There was no law then, and no semblance of order or stability. Both Scotland and England were in the melting pot, the land divided and subdivided into sundry kingdoms which flourished and died and flourished again. The people who populated them were a mixture of different strains and races: Picts and Scots from the north, Vikings from the east, Angles and Britons from the south. And it was out of this unlikely miscellany that the twin nations of England and Scotland began slowly, very slowly to emerge. The land was tailor-made for brigandry, and even landowner and freebooter on the Border made full use of it. In addition to being adept at farming and cattle-raising, the Borderer, if he intended to survive, needed to be a dab hand at murder, guerilla warfare, ambush and blackmail. In fact, the very word 'blackmail' comes from the Border counties, and every aspect of modern organized crime was practised here for more than 300 years. The daring deeds and extravagant beauties of Sir Walter Scott's stories make up a marvellous picture of a proud and independent land. But the truth was not really like that. The truth meant learning to steal as you learned to walk, doing unto your neighbour before your neighbour did unto you. This was the arena in which two warlike peoples settled their differences, and not surprisingly, the inhabitants who lived in it were fashioned by discord and continual slaughter. For century after century, the boundary line shifted and changed with successive battles until slowly, out of the confusion, it began to stabilize, become solid and unmovable, and bit by bit, the Border was at last established. But by then, subtle differences had emerged, differences you can sense even today. The line had become the divider, not merely of separate countries, but seperate nations too. And as I squelched along the muddy bank of the river Sark, I saw ahead of me through the driving rain the first place I would notice this separation – the glistening rooftops of Gretna Green.

2

Marriage Border-Style

In one sense, it is a shame that Gretna Green is the first place you come to on the Border, for it is such a drab, dour little spot, and I am sure it had never looked more drab or more dour than on that wet and windy afternoon when, drenched to the skin, I wandered into it from the southern end. Rows of little rainsoaked houses seemed to huddle together for comfort and warmth. Telephone cables hung mournfully like dripping shrouds in a horror film. Flat fields flowed off to the right, touched here and there with wisps of drifting mist.

The rain was coming through my parka hood. My feet slurped inside my boots. I was in no mood to be charitable, and Gretna Green seemed a dreary place with no trace at all of the romantic and colourful legends which surrounded it. I remember thinking: is this *it*? Is this the famous Scottish mecca of runaway marriages? Is this the village which conjurs up visions of amorous fancy? I had a mental image of eloping youngsters hotly pursued by furious mums and dads. Was this what they ran to, these cheerless little slate-grey houses, this rainsoaked street? Where were the scenic cottages I had pictured in my mind? And most important of all, where was the famous blacksmith shop where for generations couples were united in lawful – if not holy – matrimony?

I recalled a short paragraph from Pennents *Tour of Scotland* dated 1780.

"At a little distance from the bridge," it said, "stop at the little village of Gretna, the resort of all amorous couples, whose union the prudence of parents or guardians prohibits: here the young pair may be instantly united by a fisherman, a joiner, or a blacksmith, who marry from two guineas a job, to a dram of whiskey."

The writer goes on to add: "If the pursuit of friends proves very hot, and there is not time for the ceremony, the frightened pair are advised to slip into bed, are shewn to the pursuers, who imagining that they are irrecoverably united, retire and leave them to consummate their unfinished loves."

Ah yes, Gretna has a reputation all right. A brash and bawdy one. But over the years, its taste for fleshly pleasures had evidently mellowed, for the only person to greet me on that grey rainy afternoon was one old lady collecting her milk. I asked her where the smithy was. She peered at me doubtfully.

"Which smithy?" she asked.

I raised my eyebrows in surprise.

"Well, there must be a smithy," I said, "Gretna Green's always had a smithy."

"Oh aye," she said, "I meant which one d'ye want? We've got the smithy up the street, or the smithy behind the hotel."

I stared at her in dismay.

"I want the original one," I cried, "the 'world-famous one-and-only' one."

She sniffed.   "Och," she said, "we've got two o'them."

"What? Two 'one-and-only's?' "

"Oh aye."

I felt an odd sense of betrayal. It was not right. Here I was on the first step of my journey, and already I had run into the makings of a typical tourist trap. When I got to the top of the street, my worst fears proved justified. Gretna Green seemed to be bristling with 'one-and-only's'. A card pointing out the location of the blacksmith's shop had a footnote at its bottom: "Do not be misled," it said, "It has no connection with the one opened as recently as 1938".

Across the street, coachloads of tourists were disembarking on to a wide carpark. Watching them, apparently oblivious to the wind and rain, a splendid tartanned piper was blowing his lungs out, going through the cycle of usual Scottish favourites from "Road to the Isles" to "Blue Bonnets Over The Border".

The visitors evidently loved it. They bustled around, taking snapshots, bellowing at the children, buying ice-cream and peering speculatively through the windows of the Tartan and Tweed Shop.

And there, perched on the corner, flanked on one side by green fields and on the other by the cubic ultra-modern lines of the Auld Smiddy Restaurant, stood the building I was looking for: a low-roofed whitewashed bungalow with a big sign which read: 'This is the World-Famous Old Blacksmith's Shop, Marriage Room, Gretna Green.'

So this was Gretna. Home of weddings, blacksmiths, elopements and romance. It looked as if the twentieth century had landed on it with a bang. And from a great height. And yet, the interesting thing is, Gretna Green's reputation was largely achieved by accident. Before Lord Hardwicke's Marriage Act was passed in 1754, Britain was a very different country indeed. There was an easy-come easy-go attitude toward the mating business then. To get married, all you had to do was state in front of two witnesses that such-and-such a woman was your wife. And that was it. You were a bridegroom. No speeches. No involved ceremonies. No morning suits, taxis, unwanted guests. And if it did not work out, no maintenance payments either. But Lord Hardwicke's Act fixed all that when it became the Law of England on 26th March, banning all weddings which were not official. Since the law did not apply to Scotland, if a girl's parents did not approve of the way her young man dressed, or his hair-style, or the contents of his pockets, the couple simply nipped smartly over the Border, went through a primitive marriage ritual performed by a tradesman in the nearest village, usually the blacksmith over his anvil, and came back with the certificate to prove it.

That was how the whole thing began: young lovers south of the Border, unable to marry or to obtain parental consent began to flock north in their thousands and Scotland found it had a built-in biological tourist attraction as far back as the eighteenth century.

Now Gretna Green in those days was not on the main road from England at all. In other words, Gretna lost a lot of the marriage trade to the more accessible village of Springfield. But in 1830 a new road made Gretna Green the first village over the Border and cut out Springfield altogether. Gretna Green quickly moved into its boom era. The job of marrying couples off was seen as a highly lucrative business, and some of the local worthies set themselves up as unofficial 'priests'. But do not imagine for one minute that the village's new-found prosperity was welcomed by everyone. The Church was far from happy about it, and there were continual protests from local inhabitants who considered the marriage trade both immoral and disgusting.

If you look in the early eighteenth-century records of Gretna Kirk Sessions, you will see that on one particular occasion, seven people were rebuked for going through unofficial marriage ceremonies and were each fined half-a-guinea.

Most of the wedding trade in those early days was monopolized by the old Toll House and Gretna Hall. One of the early toll 'priests' was stonemason John Murray who really began to coin it in after the construction of a new bridge over the Sark in 1818, performing somewhere between six and seven thousand marriages in all. In 1854, he married a twelve year-old girl to her music master, with whom she'd eloped from Appleby. The marriage didn't last very long as it happened, because as soon as the couple crossed the Border, the bridegroom was arrested and sentenced to nine months' imprisonment at Carlisle Assizes for abduction.

Another notorious elopement took place in 1826 when Ellen Turner, a fifteen year-old heiress, was seduced by a wily bachelor called Edward Gibbon Wakefield. Wakefield managed to convince Ellen that her father was fleeing from creditors and was desperately ill. He had himself, he said, lent her father £60,000, and the only way to save the family name was to offer herself as recompense. In other words, suffer the traditional 'fate worse than death'.

The couple were married at Gretna in a makeshift ceremony and Edward whisked his new bride off to the Continent. Like all good melodramas, justice triumphed in the end, for the girl's family caught up with the couple in France. Edward was sentenced to three years in prison and the marriage was annulled by a special Act of Parliament.

But it was escapades like this which roused the wrath and indignation of the righteous citizens of the area: the laxity of Scottish law was being put to such energetic use by visitors from the south that on 21st May 1856, a public meeting was held in Carlisle to suppress once and for all the Gretna-Green weddings.

The result was the passing later that year of the Lord Brougham Act which made it a provision that anyone wishing to get married in Scotland had to first dwell in that country for a minimum of three weeks. Whatever they expected to gain by such a stipulation, it had little effect upon the steady flood of elopers. Marriage ceremonies continued thick and furious, and Gretna Green remained the centre for the runaway weddings of Europe.

All through the latter part of the nineteeth and the beginning of the twentieth century, the swelling numbers of runaway weddings continued to arouse the concern of the Church. Finally, after immense pressure, an Act of Parliament was passed in 1940 abolishing irregular marriages in Scotland for evermore. Now you would have thought that, after such drastic action, the attraction of Gretna Green would disappear, and since it has no other distinguishing features, the village would vanish completely from the tourist map. Not a bit of it. A curious situation had developed. Although the blacksmith was no longer empowered to wed anyone, the legal age for marriage without consent in Scotland was only sixteen, whereas in the rest of Britain, and in many European countries too, it was twenty-one. So the flood of runaways went on and for another thirty years Gretna continued to gain world-wide publicity.

But the final death knell for the village as a marriage centre was sounded on New Year's Day 1970, when the Law of England was altered to reduce the legal age of marriage without parent's consent from twenty-one to eighteen. This new Bill had a drastic effect on the number of elopers, for it meant that couples over seventeen had only a short time to wait before getting married legally anywhere they chose. Gretna's weddings understandably dropped from 521 in 1966 to only 52 five years later. And yet somehow, even today, its very name retains a compulsive charm. Although a dual-carriageway by-passes the village completely, tourists flock here in droves, both summer and winter. To them, Gretna Green still means weddings and romance, and with its blacksmiths' shops, tartanned pipers, teahouses and curio stalls, the village does not intend to let them forget it.

It seemed daft somehow to come to Gretna Green and *not* visit the blacksmith shop, so I wandered over, paid my fivepence and was hustled through the turnstile. The custodian turned out to be a cheerful pink-cheeked Scot who until four years ago had been a foreman in a chipboard factory, Syd Hannah. We stood in his souvenir shop, formerly the blacksmith's cottage, and he told me about the throngs of sightseers who descend on him day in, day out.

"If there's a party of twenty or so," he said, "We put on one of our mock wedding ceremonies."

"But does anyone ever arrive expecting to be *really* married?" I asked.

"Oh aye," he said, "all the time. Ye'll get them coming through the door, they'll come into the shop an' ask: 'Is the 'priest' aboot?' And one o' the girls will say: 'You mean Mr Hannah.' Then they ask me t' marry them."

"What do you do?"

He shrugged.

"What can I do? Send them packing, that's what. The Registrar's office is two miles up the road. If they look old enough, I send them there. But I would say a good percentage o' them are under sixteen, which means they're too young even for Scottish law, so the Registrar'll not be able to help them much."

"What sort of state are they in?" I asked.

He scratched his elbow thoughtfully.

"Dishevelled and very, very frightened," he said, "Nearly all o' them are like that, little bags of rag and bone. I feel sorry for them, but what good is feeling sorry? They look surprised when ye tell them the law changed years ago. Funny, isn't it, the way the old legend's stuck."

I peered around the crowded shop, at the brass medallions and copper kettles, the long coaching horns and tartan purses, and line upon line of picture postcards. The sound of bagpipes split the air outside, and in shuffled a fresh batch of tourists. They wandered about in dribs and drabs, Americans mostly, poking among the miniature pots and cauldrons, the little kilted dolls, the brass beermugs and tartan pennants, arguing and bargaining, clucking and clattering, rattling their money and shooting off their flash-bulbs the way Americans inevitably do. There was an air of frenzied gaiety about the place that seemed a complete contrast to the rain and wind outside.

I strolled into the blacksmith's shop proper, and watched Syd go through one of his mock wedding ceremonies. The ceiling was low, the oak beams lined with upturned horseshoes. Photographs and paintings of famous Gretna Green characters peered down from the whitewashed walls. In the centre of the room stood the worn remains of part of an ancient tree, and perched on this was the famous old anvil. I watched Syd decorating it with meticulous care, laying out a huge iron hammer and a long-barrelled shotgun. He presented one of the American ladies with a veil and bouquet, and one of the men with a smart grey topper. Grinning and chuckling, the rest of the party shuffled in behind, and with an air of jocular authority, Syd's ritual began.

It was all very tongue-in-cheek and the jokes were dreadful. But Syd delivered them with such panache the audience loved it. There was no doubt at all that he had the instinctive flair of a born comedian. Whenever the laughter subsided even for a moment, his sheer exhuberance started it off again.

One of his lady assistants brought me a welcome cup of tea, and I stood in the corner sipping gratefully as the Americans filed happily out, and the next group trickled in. Syd's tireless energy was beginning to conquer even me. In spite of my sour mood, I was enjoying myself at last.

I said goodbye to Syd eventually, wandered into the Auld Smiddy snack bar and ordered scones and tea. The scones were stale, the tea was cold. My sense of dejection returned. I sat peering through the drizzle-streaked windows at the visitors who bartered, bounced and bustled. Fresh coachloads rumbled in. I was caught up in the tinsel and trappings of the very tourist trails I had tried so hard to escape. With a sigh, I called the waitress and paid my bill.

The rain was slackening as I wandered out of town and back to the river. I clambered over a wire fence and began to follow the Sark's grassy banks. White cattle eyed me dubiously through the drizzly mid-afternoon moisture. Buttercups cluttered the field in splashes of brilliant colour. There were fresh pasturelands ahead, soft woodlands and distant hills. The commercialism and confusion of Gretna lay behind me. It was brash and it was fun, but it was not what I had come to see. After the non-stop tinkle of cash-registers, it felt good to get back to the clean Border air.

3

Frontier Justice

Curious things, Borders: a bit like people in a way, always rushing off at tangents for no rhyme or reason. Following the line during the first part of the hike had proved easy for it travelled straight up the middle of the river Sark. But a few miles east of Gretna it suddenly twisted without warning and set off straight as a plumbline up a steep grassy field which swelled against the sky like the crest of an ocean wave. It took me a good ten minutes to ford the river, for it was swollen with rain and I did not relish the thought of wading it, particularly in clothes just beginning to thaw after the morning's deluge. Besides, the rain had stopped at last, and over east the sky seemed to be breaking up, sending through shafts of thin watery-gold sunlight.

I scrambled up the grassy bank with a new sense of optimism. Woolly-flanked sheep darted nervously from my path, and along the skyline a flock of dairy cows came nudging nosily down to meet me. I filled my lungs with air, smelling the good after-rain scent of fresh blossom and sun-warmed pine. To my right stood a water meadow scattered with wild flowers. In front, tall trees traced a narrow line between rich cornfields and I knew that somewhere in that maze of undergrowth, shrouded with nettles, scrub and twisted overhanging branches, I would find a narrow ditch, less than six feet deep, three feet wide and three miles long: Scots Dyke, the longest man-made barrier on the Border.

I peered at the countryside around me. So this was the 'debatable land'. It looked so peaceful, so green and tranquil. Soft fields dipped and rolled in a soothing undulating rhythm. Rivers slid silently between boulder-studded meadows. Farmhouses clustered pasture-folds and cattle stood straight and immobile, caught in the stillness of the early summer evening.

I listened to the sounds of wrens and chaffinches, and the far-off, almost imperceptable rumble of a lazy tractor. And yet ... the spot on which I was standing, the very spot, was once the centre of one of the most extraordinary sections of countryside in history. This was Britain's 'badman's territory'.

There are those who will tell you that the whole Border was 'debatable land', but this is not true. There is only one section which was *the* 'debatable land', the region bounded on the south by the Esk Estuary, on the east by the Esk and Liddell, on the west by the river Sark and on the north by Tarras Moss. In the fifteenth century, no-one really knew who this area belonged to, and both Scotland and England were loath to accept responsibility for policing it. Oh, they wanted it all right; or at least, they wanted the nearby wealthy monastery at Canonbie. But the prospect of bringing order to such an unadministerable province was so daunting that neither country would accept it. Nor, on the other hand, were they prepared to let the other side have it, and for generation after generation, the 'debatable land' remained a thorn in the sides of both governments. It was a hotbed of violence. Its unsettled nature attracted the worst elements of society. Murder and arson were casual everyday occurrences. Dispute after dispute ravaged its twelve-mile stretch, and although the two kingdoms tried repeatedly to reach some kind of settlement, the 'debatable land' remained stubbornly debatable.

One method of dealing with the criminal element – a rather extreme one – was to devastate the countryside, and this was done regularly. But the scavengers who inhabited the area were migrant by nature: they simply moved out when a purge began and moved back in again as soon as it was over.

By 1551, both countries had come to the end of their tether. The 'debatable land', they decided, was simply 'ungovernable'. How could you impose law on a people who saw law as a social disgrace, who moved about the landscape like flitting shadows? A charter was drawn up – a most remarkable charter – turning the 'debatable land' into 'no-man's land'. It stated clearly that anyone would be free to rob, burn, plunder and kill within its boundaries without being held liable to law. Now that may seem an extraordinary step for civilized governments to take, even in such uncivilized times, but the idea was to so sicken the inhabitants with violence that they would, by choice, come to heel or clear out altogether.

The idea misfired. Far from being sickened, the freebooters of the frontier actually thrived on their new freedom, and within months the crime rate had reached an unimaginable high.

Clearly, neither Scotland nor England could ignore the situation any longer. Order had to be established, responsibilities designated. In 1552, the two countries came together to decide once and for all where the Border should go. Even then, their troubles were not over. The English Warden drew his line too far north, the Scottish Warden drew his too far south. In the end, they had to call in the French Ambassador to settle the affair. He drew a line straight up the middle, and that is where the ditch was dug, to mark plainly and for all time the division between both nations. Scots Dyke it was called, and you can still walk along it today, from the river Sark to the River Esk.

I ought to explain at this point, I think, who these Wardens were and what their function was, because really it was the Wardens – and the territory they patrolled – which made the Border such a unique place. I keep talking about the Border as if it resembled America's Wild West, but when you come right down to it, that is not such an outlandish comparison. They had the lot on the Border: the rustlers and cattle barons, the trail towns and stage lines, the bandits, the savages, the carpetbaggers. They even had their own equivalent of the U.S. marshals, because that, in a nutshell is what the Wardens of the Marches represented: law and order. It was their job to bring stability, to establish peace, to administer justice. Not that they ever did, mind you, not in any true sense. My God, you only have to look at the enormity of that task. Britain herself was far from civilized – or at least, her civilization took a cruder form than the one we understand today – and here on the Border you had vast sections of unfenced country inhabited by people whose customs of murder and savagery dated back centuries. On top of that, here was a convenient frontier line offering a sanctuary for any lawbreaker who cared to use it. How could anyone bring peace and justice to such an area? I do not believe the Wardens were ever intended to be the perfect answer. They were simply a stop-gap, an attempt to maintain a skeletal structure of order, a last-ditch barrier against anarchy.

There were six of them in all, three on each side of the line. Actually, there were seven in the end, for Liddesdale was considered so warlike that it needed a Warden of its own, but the original plan was for six, governing the East, Middle and West Marches. They were paid around £1000 a year which, even in those days, seems a measly sum for such a responsible appointment. But it had its compensations. It was a job that carried a lot of perks. Power, for one thing. The Warden and his family represented the only authority on the frontier, which meant he was free to dispense justice as he saw fit, and power, to certain types of men can be a lot more precious than money. But the Warden did not do too badly on the economic side either. He was entitled by law to confiscate the goods and livestocks of convicted criminals, and he often managed to pick up a pound or two on land grants and other payments. In return for this, he was expected to suppress crime, to hold international courts with his opposite number over the Border and to co-operate with him in pursuing and arresting raiders who had crossed the line. All of which may seem fairly straightforward until you remember that Scotland and England were as often at war as at peace, and if law had been brought to the frontier it was an uneasy law, broken frequently by the Wardens themselves who were constantly at each other's throats. Imagine trying to reason, parley and administer justice with a man you considered to be your greatest enemy on earth. And of course that is precisely how they must have felt. As Warden of the March, a man became the supreme commander in his own area. He was answerable only to London or Edinburgh, and in those days, London at least was like the other side of the world. He held in his hand the lives and destinies of all the people who lived nearby. His only rival, the only man who could approach him in terms of power and authority was his opposite number on the other side of the Border. It is not surprising that the English and Scottish Wardens saw each other as potential adversaries rather than allies.

The Wardens' Courts had seemed a marvellous idea on paper, but when they were put into practice they frequently dissolved into unseemly brawls. There was the famous fray at Redeswire in 1575 when half-way through the court proceedings the two Wardens began insulting each other. The precise cause of their argument was never established, but it did not take long before the retainers on both sides were going at it hammer and tongs. It ended with dead bodies all over the place and the English Warden being taken prisoner.

The Redeswire affair was a celebrated one, but it was by no means exceptional. The Wardens too often found direct action more effective than the negotiating table. A perfect example is Buccleuch's raid on Carlisle Castle to rescue Kinmont Willie. They were doing a tough job in a tough land, and like the marshals of the old west, their methods were often tough too. It was not just the freebooters and moss troopers who turned the Border into a lawless paradise, it was the very law-makers themselves, the men who were meant to be imposing and enforcing codes of conduct, principles and statutes. Real law took centuries to establish. First, the killing and pillaging had to burn itself out, and even then, the inherent sense of bitterness and petty hatred which had grown up among the old Border families had to fade sufficiently to allow peace and order to be generated.

True, with the digging of Scots Dyke, the 'debatable land' lost some of its lawless appeal, but only in the sense that it now became absorbed into the rest of the Border. The nature of the land did not change. Laws existed, but only on paper. A wily criminal with his wits about him could still lead a highly lucrative life and look forward to a comfortable retirement or a peaceful death in bed. If you were unfortunate enough to be brought to justice, it was more likely to be the result of a personal squabble with the Warden or a member of his family than retribution for the actual offence. You had, after all, hundreds of square miles of open country to disappear into. But by the sixteenth century, a subtle change had taken place on the frontier. The lawless element was still there of course, but there had been an interesting shift in power. The outlaws had dug their heels in: no longer was it necessary to flee into the hills after a murder or raid. There was no longer anything to flee from. The big outlaw families could match the Wardens in strength and man-power any day of the week, and the Border had fallen into the grip of organized crime. In the sixteenth century, this was gangster country, home of the syndicate, the mob, the protection racket. Among the early 'godfathers', one of the most famous was Johnnie Armstrong, a kind of cross between Lucky Luciano and Al Capone. I do not know why it is, but historians and ballad writers always seem to paint history's outlandish characters in their brightest colours. Armstrong has been lamented in legend and song as if he had been some kind of Robin Hood, and yet, he was a tyrant in every sense of the word. He spread a web of corruption along the entire Esk Valley. Every householder from Langholm to the sea had to pay him protection money for the privilege of staying alive.

Like the big hoodlum chiefs of Chicago in the twenties, Armstrong was able to laugh at authority. The Wardens of the Marches were helpless against him. They had neither the arms nor the men to take him on in open battle. The English Warden sent repeated protests to Scotland's James V, but year after year Armstrong went on despoiling the Border with contemptuous indifference for lawmen on either side.

Eventually however, the Scottish king decided that the outrages had gone on long enough. In June 1529 he sent word to Armstrong to meet him for parley at Carlin Rigg. There is no doubt that Armstrong was expecting to be rewarded rather than punished, for it had always been the English side of the Border he had laid waste, never the Scottish. Up he trooped with thirty-six of his scavengers, all decked out in their most extravagant finery. His display was meant primarily to impress James, but it was the biggest mistake he could have made. The King, seeing Armstrong's mobsters arrayed in such splendour, flew into a fury and made his famous exclamation, "What wants that knave that a king should have?" He ordered Armstrong and his followers to be executed at once. Like most tyrants, Armstrong found the fruits of his labours too lucrative to give up without a fight and for several hours he pleaded desperately for his life. He protested that he had never killed a single Scot. He swore continual devotion to the Scottish throne. He offered to kidnap any English nobleman the King might name. But James was not having any. Armstrong and his men were strung up peremptorily from nearby trees.

Scottish poets persist in seeing Johnnie Armstrong as a splendid fellow martyred by the force of circumstances, but in truth he was a callous, brutal killer. Just as the indictment of Al Capone was a turning point in Chicago's fight against crime, Armstrong's death became a milestone in the struggle for law and order on the Border. Other outlaw families came to see that their immunity could not last for ever, that although they continued to exist as mini-gods in their own territories, they were not invincible, there were other forces more powerful, men determined to see that justice would at last prevail.

The Armstrongs continued to stick to their original lifestyle of robbery, arson and murder, but it is difficult not to feel a sneaking regard for their cheek. They were one of the most flamboyant of the Border families. Their reputation, and their livelihood was based largely on what they could grab by sheer force, but they did it with such flair and such swagger that somehow you recall their exploits as being colourful rather than brutal.

Of all the Armstrongs, I think my favourite was Archie Armstrong who was arrested for sheep stealing and sentenced to death in Jedburgh by James VI. In the courtroom he pleaded that he was an ignorant fellow who had just heard of the Bible, and who would like to read it through for the benefit of his soul if the King would be so good as to spare him the time. The King was amused by Archie and instead of hanging him, took him on as Court Jester, a most enviable position in those days. But Archie's witticisms turned out to be so impudent and outrageous that in the end James was obliged to give him the sack. Archie was certainly the only Armstrong to become a legend, not for his savagery, but for his sense of humour.

They turned out to be a hard push, those three miles up Scots Dyke. For one thing, it had rained so hard that the ditch was running with water, and for another, the undergrowth had become so thick that I felt I was caught in an endless jungle. My nostrils filled with the soggy odour of dank scrub. Birdsong jangled in my ears. Kamikaze midges nose-dived my face. Through the trees I caught occasional glimpses of a sunlit sky, but in my tight little claustrophic world, bush and scrub enveloped me like a vice. Clump, clump, clump, shove, shove, shove, I fought my way through that maddening, stifling, cluttering, smothering thicket like Stanley in the Congo, pausing only to slap at the flies or castigate the birds with a string of curses. Sweat ran from my pores in what seemed bucketfuls, and I regretted my decision to follow the ditch itself, thinking longingly of the track I had seen running across the ploughed field to my left.

I pushed against the overhanging curtain of branches with a sense of hot frustration. The day was dwindling and I was moving too slowly. I felt, in the confinement of my mind, as if I was fighting for every step. For a short while the bushes thinned out, and I was able to move freely between the scattered tree-trunks, but then the scrub crept in as thick as ever and it was back to the push and pull, wriggle and strain and heave.

It was forty minutes later when I finally pushed my way through the last section of Scots Dyke and burst into the open with an overwhelming sense of relief. I was out. Out, out, out, out. And the sun was shining, or at least it *had* been shining, for it was now mid-evening. But the heavy bank of cloud had broken up, leaving just a few fleecy bits of pale fluff scudding westward across an otherwise faultless sky. I slithered down the muddy cart-track, delighted to be free of the thicket at last. My clothes were littered with bits of green, and my hair lay plastered with sweat on my forehead. Below, the fields slid gently down to the sweeping curve of the river Esk. The Esk, the Esk, the glorious Esk.

I tumbled down its steep bluffs gratefully to wash my face in the rushing stream. Who would have believed, I thought, that a day which began so menacingly could end with such peace? Water rippled over white boulders, polished by the sun. On the opposite bank, a pair of shiny-flanked horses perched like book-ends, rump to rump. Trees hovered close to the water's edge, their branches lifting in the soft summer breeze.

I took off my boots and bathed my feet in the rippling river. The water felt ice-cold. I dried between my toes, pulled my boots back on and clambered up. The current at this point was fast but not deep, and out in the centre of the stream stood a solitary angler, casting his line. What a picture he made with the fading sun behind him. I wandered down to get a closer look, and sitting at the river's edge, eating an apple, I spotted a second angler, all decked out in waders and neat little tweed hat.

"Hello," he said, "come far?"

"Solway Firth," I grunted, flopping down beside him on the rocks. He was a small man with a very red face, and the corners of his mouth were turned inward at each end so that he seemed to be perpetually smiling.

"Good fishing?" I asked casually.

He grinned.

"The best there is," he said, "Salmon and sea-trout mostly, but you won't find a better river in all of southern Scotland, unless it's the Tweed."

He finished his apple and tossed the core into the shallows.

"Fisherman yourself?" he asked.

I shook my head hastily.

"No, no, I know nothing about it at all."

He chuckled.

"Oh well, maybe you're better off."

We sat for a while with the fading sun in our faces, watching the man in the stream reel in his line. In the stillness of the evening, it made a sound like the chatter of a distant tommy gun. On the opposite bank, the horses lifted their heads curiously, nostrils flared.

I stretched myself out, leaning back with my head against my pack.

"I suppose it's a big thing in Scotland, fishing," I murmured conversationally.

The man beside me gave a short laugh.

"Not just Scotland," he said, "Angling is a big thing all over the British Isles. It's the country's number one sport."

"You're joking," I said.

He shook his head.

"There are more than four million anglers in Britain today," he stated, "It's a two hundred million pound industry."

In the grass at his side stood his little box of flies. I peered into it, poking at the bits of feather and wire.

"What's this?" I asked.

"That's a Silver March Brown," he said authoratively.

"And this?"

"A Blue Charm."

"This?"

"A Greenwell's Glory."

"You mean every one has its own name?"

"Right. And its own use too. Choosing the right fly at the right time is very, very important. You see, waterborn flies aren't like household flies. They spend the first part of their lives under the river where they're known as nymphs. Later on, they swim up to the surface and shed their outer skin. Now the fly fisherman looks to see what kind of fly is hatching. Flies generally live no more than a couple of days, see. Some, like the may fly, last only an hour or two. So it's no good sticking the wrong one on the end of your line because the fish will know at a glance that it's a dud."

I frowned.

"Well, how do you know which *is* the right fly?"

"By keeping your eyes peeled. Watch for the flies on the surface, see how they change as the day goes on. Make sure you cast with a fly that the fish knows is likely to be around at that particular time. But that's not the only thing: the condition of the river, the state of the weather, the presence or absence of sunshine, these are all factors which come into determining the kind of fly you use."

"Sounds complicated," I said.

He shrugged.

"Well, it takes a bit of experience. Mind you, I'm talking about trout fishing. It doesn't really matter what fly you use for salmon because they eat nothing from the time they enter fresh water until they return to sea."

"In that case," I said, "why do they take the fly?"

He smiled.

"That's something nobody rightly knows," he answered, "Maybe they just do it out of irritation."

Somewhere in the treetops an owl hooted mournfully. I heard a dog yap as cattle were driven from a nearby field. There was a sense of subtle stillness, a feeling that in a moment or two the river, and the trees along its banks, would be shrouded by night. None of this seemed to occur to the fisherman out in the stream. He stood still as a boulder, oblivious to everything around him.

"Your friend seems in a different world," I whispered.

The little man laughed.

"That's the funny thing about fishing," he said, "It doesn't matter where you do it or who you do it with, you're always alone. It's an aloneness of the mind. Understand?"

I nodded absently. I was watching the man in the centre of the stream who had suddenly begun to move. He twitched his rod in a series of flicks so that the line went streaming out like a whiplash, streaking further and further with each successive movement.

"What's he doing?" I asked.

The little man leaned forward, watching closely.

"He's spotted a fish, I think," he said, "He's casting slightly upstream of where he thinks it's lying, letting the fly float past him so he can take it on the rise."

"But how can he guarantee to hit the right spot?"

"That's the fun of it. A real fly fisherman will spend hours on end practising a cast like that. It's an art in itself."

I watched the fisherman flick for the final time. A ripple ran along the line, taking it a foot or two further out and then, light as thistledown, the fly settled on the surface.

"I don't understand," I said, "how that tiny bit of feather and wire can carry the line so far."

"Oh, it's not the fly that does it," he explained, "It's the weight of the line itself. By casting in a series of movements, letting out more and more line with each flick, he can throw it twenty to thirty yards."

"Doesn't he find it boring, just standing there?"

He began to laugh.

"I admit it takes a certain kind of temperament to care about angling," he said, "but boring? No, never boring. I go for it because I go for excitement."

"Excitement?" I echoed doubtfully, listening to the gentle murmur of the river and the far-off whisper of the trees.

"Well, it's basically an inner excitement I'm talking about," he said, "For instance, if you were to watch me catch a pike of say fifteen pounds, it would be exciting for you to see the hooking and the landing of that pike, but only for the time it took to catch it. Now for me, that excitement would have lasted for four or five hours. In a nutshell, that's what angling's all about."

I sat waiting for the thrill of the catch, but either my man had mis-cast or the fish had been warier than he had thought. In any event, nothing happened, and after chatting a while longer I said goodbye and made my way up the river bluffs looking for somewhere to camp.

It seems idiotic, but fishing on the Esk once caused one of the bitterest, longest-running and most incongruous disputes ever to arise between England and Scotland. The Esk was always noted for its fine salmon, and in the 1400s, the English erected a fish garth or enclosure to trap the fish as they moved upstream to spawn. The Scots were not too happy about the idea, because they felt they were being deprived of lots of plump succulent food so they crossed the Border and tore it down. The English, piqued, built it up again. The Scots promptly re-demolished it. And so it went on for nearly three-quarters of a century, each side amusing itself by either building the fish garth up, or pulling it down. The matter went to extraordinary lengths. In 1474, it came under discussion at Westminster and a Commission was appointed to get the thing ironed out. It was not very successful evidently because in 1485 another Commission had to be set up. Two years later, a third Commission swung into action, but still the fish garth dispute went stubbornly on. The affair finally reached such proportions that King James of Scotland challenged the Earl of Surrey to a personal duel.

"Single combat," he said, "The stakes to be the restoration of Berwick to Scotland, and the removal of the fish garth."

Surrey declined because, as he pointed out, it was unlikely the English king would ratify such a wager, whatever the outcome. The episode was resolved at last in 1543, but how, or on what terms, is no longer known.

I swung right, leaving the Esk behind and following the line of the river Liddel. It was already dusk by the time I found a good level spot and got my tent up. I rummaged about in the brush, found some twigs that had somehow dodged the morning's downpour and started a tiny fire. I stuck a can of beer in the river shallows to cool, then heated some ravioli in my metal pot and roasted a few hot dogs on long green twigs in the moonlight.

By the time I had finished supper, darkness had wrapped itself around me like a great woolly glove. Only the river remained clear. It lay shining like a soft pale canyon lit with a strange fluorescent glow, while all around it the world settled into an indistinct blur of greys, blues and blacks.

The beer was chilled when I dug it out of the water. I sat on the bluffs and unlaced my boots, caught in the illusion that I was the only human being left alive.

Tomorrow, I thought, I would leave the rural tracks behind and reach the real Border, the wild hills and rugged country that formed the hackles and the backbone of Britain.

Somewhere over east a night owl hooted sadly. I was filled with a sense of luxurious peace as I washed my pot in the river, unzipped my sleeping bag and wriggled into bed.

Gretna Green: the Old Blacksmith's Shop

Forestry plantations in Northumberland

Logs in the Border Forest waiting for transportation to the pulp mills

Bellingham Village

Cuddy's Well at Bellingham, where St Cuthbert is said to have baptized converts. The water is believed to have miraculous powers

The Long Pack grave in Bellingham churchyard, key to an ancient mystery

Kielder Castle: headquarters of the Forestry Commission

Kielder Viaduct, the finest example of a skew bridge in Britain

Kielder village

South of Kielder—part of the valley soon to be flooded to provide
a reservoir

The Border abounds with wild life—deer are a common sight in the
forest areas

Logging roads make the going easy through the Border Forest

4

The Big Forest

Wild geese woke me early in the morning, and I scrambled from my tent and peered around at one of the most beautiful days I had ever seen. Not a cloud marred the sky, and even at that early hour the sun's rays struck through my wool shirt with a friendly glow. Grey rocks clustered the river's edge and the trees looked fresh and new and incredibly lush as if I had somehow missed their colour the day before.

I ran along the bank like a schoolboy, yahoooing and yodellahing, my feet chilled by the heavy dew. I found a deep rocky pool, and tearing off my clothes plunged into it without a moment's thought, stark naked. Arrrrgh-arrrrgh, I screamed, regretting such rashness instantly as the freezing water folded around me. Ah ah ah ah ah ah ah. Gasping and spluttering, I began to splash as vigorously as I could. It was no use. My new-found elation was snuffed out like a candleflame. Even on warm sunny mornings, the Liddel was not designed for pre-breakfast baths. Never again, I swore to myself, never, never, never again would I submit my poor skin and bone to such appalling treatment.

I towelled myself down, pulled on my clothes and, shivering profusely, re-kindled the fire. I used a boy-scout trick which is worth a mention. If you have had a good blaze going the night before, don't stamp it out: try this. When you first build your fire, cut out a square patch of turf about two inches deep, and keep the flames inside the hole. When the time comes to go to bed, spread the cinders out and criss-cross them with green twigs. Then re-place the turf as carefully as you can, using soil and stones to plug up any gaps. Make sure no air can find its way in. Next morning, remove the turf, fan the embers with a tin plate or hat, and with luck they should burst into flame. Do not however, whatever you do, use this trick when there are trees within twenty or thirty feet because heat can travel under the soil, and of course – although I am sure there is no need to mention this – always see that your fire is well and truly out when leaving.

I gobbled down breakfast as fast as I could: hot dog sandwiches and a mug of tea. Then I dismantled the tent, cleared up the site and set off along the riverbank toward the hazy blue sweep of the distant hills. I was stiffer than I had expected, and both calves and the little slivers of muscle down the front of my shins jounced painfully with each step. One of the main problems with long-distance walking is that you build up a kind of accumulative tiredness. You set off the first day feeling vigorous and fresh: the next, you're just a teeny bit less enthusiastic: the next even less so, until by the end of a week, unless you've worked up some sort of rhythm, your body feels drained and way-worn.

After a couple of miles I made a further depressing discovery. There was a nail sticking up inside my boot. It was too far in to flatten with a stone, and I was obliged to stick a tenpenny piece over it, and fasten it in place with a strip of elastoplast. That brought some improvement, but I went on my way with an unwieldy lump under my big toe, and no prospect of a cobbler for at least another three days.

As I plodded steadily eastward, the nature of the countryside began to change. First, the flatness of the early stretches gave way to a kind of ragged roughness, as if the landscape had begun to toss like an angry sea. Distance and perspective seemed to thrust themselves upon me, bringing a new kind of remoteness. I was filled with an overpowering sense of space. There was room here. Lots of room. Room enough, you felt, for the whole wide world to lose itself.

Straggling strips of pine came crawling down the gullies, and as I moved higher, the forest thickened until soon all the isolated patches had merged into one, a huge spreading carpet of treetops that curled up the valleys and ran over the hills like welsh rarebit. I had entered the Border Forest, the largest man-made forest in Europe, 400 square miles of Scots pine, sitka and Norway spruce, hemlock, Lawson cypress and Douglas fir.

It is not possible to walk the Border without being aware of that forest. It hovers around the fells like a hungry animal, always gobbling up more. It creeps over the hillsides like cancer, cutting in roads where there were no roads, fencing off land where there were no fences, ploughing up peat and planting neat methodical rows of Christmas trees where once there was only heather and bracken and emptiness. The forest is destroying the very nature of the Border country as surely as the raiders who devastated it four hundred years ago, but in a more ingenious way. After all, how can you argue against the utilization of unproductive moorland? And yet, in a tight little overcrowded island like ours, where the one thing we do not have enough of is space to stretch out, to move around, to feel uncluttered, it does seem a shame to me that our wild hills are vanishing under tree plantations when more than ninety per cent of our timber has to be imported anyway.

Mind you, the Forestry Commission is not unsympathetic to the views of ramblers and conservationists. You can walk around the woodlands, for instance – as long as you keep to the Forestry roads, and in some of the more scenic areas, the Commission has provided picnic spots and even camp sites. But the fact remains that yet again people are being shepherded into tight little corners, and one of Britain's last stretches of wilderness is being steadily pruned away.

Still, the forest does provide employment, and I caught my first glimpse of the men who work there just after lunch, as I was following a narrow unpaved track that ripped through the conifers like a ragged tear. A group of small trucks stood parked discreetly in the bush, and through the network of branches swelled the muffled roar of power saws. Here, the Forest had suddenly vanished, as if a giant hand had scooped out a great hole in its foliage. The earth was littered with criss-crossed treetrunks interspersed with mattresses of springy spruce boughs. The whiff of fresh sap drifted in my nostrils, bringing with it vivid memories of the days in my early youth when I had worked the logging camps of the British Columbia Coastal Range.

I left the track and scrambled up the tufted hillside, picking my way through the debris of littered timber, feeling a certain smugness and disdain as I saw how puny these British trunks were compared with the great monsters we had tumbled in Canada's north-west.

The fallers were spread out across the hill, one man about every thirty yards or so. I made my way toward the nearest, a small middle-aged labourer with pepper-and-salt beard stubble, who was handling his power saw with a lack of concern that made the skin along my spine twitch. Power saws can be vicious things and I have seen dreadful accidents involving them. But when I got closer I saw that the one this man was using was small and compact, and whenever he took his finger from the trigger, the chain stopped whirring. He worked with an economy of movement, slicing through the narrow trunks like a grocer cutting cheese, and I thought with a twinge of envy of the countless hours we had spent toppling those giant British Columbia conifers, hammering in chocks to widen the cuts so that the saws could bite deeper and deeper. Eeeeeeiiiiiiiii; there was a sudden groan and the tree toppled, falling slowly at first, then crashing earthwards with a great ear-rending whooomph.

Once the trunk hit the ground, the man moved swiftly up its length scraping his power saw along the bark, trimming off the branches with neat methodical movements. Sawdust and pinechips danced in the air like sparks from a firecracker.

In less than five minutes he had whittled it smooth and was already peering around at the next one.

"What happens after you've cut them down?" I asked curiously, for the slope was literally strewn with logs.

He paused, his narrow face shiny with sweat, obviously glad of a chance to rest.

"Well, they're dragged down to the road," he grunted, "then they're barked on a mechanical peeler and sliced into short lengths on a sawbench. After that, we load them on to lorries for transport to wherever they're going."

Around us, the sound of nearby power-saws was like the drone from a thousand beehives. Every few seconds the air would be filled with shuddering row as another spruce trunk bit the dust.

"Seems a pity to see them fall," I said sadly.

The man took off his protective helmet and began to mop his glistening face. He spat on the ground, choosing his target and hitting it with expert precision.

"If we didn't do it," he growled, "the forest'd get choked to a standstill. The trees crowd each other close after fifteen or twenty years, and if we didn't thin 'em out, the good specimens would never get a chance to develop. That's why we keep trimming them out every three or four years. But we only take the poorer trees and leave the valuable ones to the last. Even so, you only find about one tree in eight lasts long enough to reach its full height."

"How do you know which trees to go for?"

"Well, if you look at any of this lot, you'll see markings on their bark. They've already been singled out by foresters. It's a highly-skilled operation, thinning is."

I sat down on the fallen log, pushing my pack on the ground in front of me.

"It's always puzzled me," I said, "how you manage to get in between them, particularly when they grow so thick and close together."

The man ran one hand through his hair.

"We've got brasher girls," he said, smiling, "Teams of women with curved knives who prune off the lower branches. It not only makes it easier to move around, it reduces the fire risk and makes for fewer knots in the timber later on."

"What's it used for, the timber?" I asked.

"All sorts of things. Pulp mills mostly. The big trees are sawn into boxboards. Some of the spruce is used in carpentry and joinery, the rest goes to a big newsprint mill in Cheshire. A lot of the wood goes to chipboard factories in Newcastle and Teeside. The straighter trunks make good pitprops, telegraph poles, tripods for hay-dryers, that sort of thing. There's quite a big demand from local farmers for fence stakes too."

I grinned at him.

"You seem to know it inside out."

He shrugged.

"I've been at it long enough," he said, "Nearly ten years. I used to work in the shipyards at Wallsend-on-Tyne, but it was such a dodgy business – you never knew whether you'd be working from one day to the next. I decided to bring the family out here. The pay's less than what I was earning, but we've got a good house that goes with the job."

"It must have taken quite an adjustment though," I said, "Coming from the city – out here."

He shook his head.

"Not really. I like to be out in the open air – I mean air that smells like air. In Wallsend, all we ever got was the stench of the boneyard at North Shields. Up here now, you smell the hills everywhere you go, and they never smell the same way twice. Ever since I was a kid I suffered from bronchitis, but since we moved to Kielder I've not had a single spot of bother. That must prove something."

"But doesn't it get lonely, living in the middle of nowhere?"

He grinned.

"That's what people from cities always think. What did we do in Wallsend that was so marvellous? Every night, down we'd plonk in front of the telly. Same old thing: box on at half-past five, off at close-down. Now when you live in a place like Kielder you make your own entertainment. The village itself is so shut off you can't afford to shut yourself off any more. You get to know your neighbour and he gets to know you, and I'll tell you this: before I came up here I didn't know what a social life was. Now I've got a house and friends all around me. My kids have colour in their cheeks and a good school to go to. You think I'd go back to that other thing, back to the shipyard? Not on your nelly. I wouldn't change this lot for any town job, not ever."

He was a pleasant little man, thin as a rake with not an ounce of muscle on his bones, but when he handled that power saw he went through the trees like a devil incarnate. I said goodbye and set off again toward the Forestry Centre at Kielder. There was a man who had his priorities right, I thought. He knew what it meant to be happy. His enthusiasm cheered me immensely, and I whistled as I jogged along, passing mile after mile of neatly-laid conifers.

After thirty minutes or so I came across an obelisk of grey sandstone, twenty feet high, all that remained of the old toll road built in 1776 to carry coal from Plashetts over to Liddesdale. The ground was open, rimmed on one side by the forest, on the other by a wide muddy bog. Not a trace of the road itself could be seen through the clumps of rippling heather. How easily the hills take

back what is their own. Man makes his paltry changes and
slowly, inexorably, the hills wipe them out.

On the side of the obelisk, I was just able to make out the
following engraving:

For horses employed in leading coals:	2d each.
All other horses:	3d each.
Cattle:	1d each.
Sheep, Calves, Swine.	$\frac{1}{2}$d each.

All afternoon, I plodded steadily along, following the jig-saw
lines of the Forestry by-ways. The trail bobbed and dipped,
skirting a riverbank, riding a hillcrest. And always the skyline
offered the same unrelieved view of pointed treetops. Somehow,
on this stretch of the Border, the forest is a presence you can
never get away from. Wherever you go, you know that it is
there. Waiting. Hiding. Ready to pounce. Even on open
hillsides, it is just around the corner, playing a game, ready to
close in again and snap you up in its grip. It can tease you, taunt
you, tickle and infuriate you. You begin to think of it as a living
force, something to be outwitted, outsmarted, dodged and
evaded. It never looks as if it belongs on the fells, that is the
thing: it is always an intruder. The trees look too new, too small,
too neat and orderly ever to have been put there by nature. No,
it is the work of man, you can see that in a glance. The forest is
like a warped penny that can never fit snugly into its ordained
slot, and yet oddly enough, the whole area was once a forest
before. Centuries ago, the entire Border was covered with
deciduous trees. There was birch, alder, rowan, willow, wych
elms, hollies, hazel, ash and lots more. A different landscape they
would have made then, softer, rounder, more luxurious – none
of the harsh prickly severity of today. But man fixed that, as
always. In the past, it was man's nature to chop forests down
rather than build them up. They were there to be used, and if
they were not used well, they got in the way. So he cleared them
out indiscriminately, either to make room for hunting, for
farming, for building, or to use as fuel and construction material.
All of which no doubt made sound common sense two or three
centuries ago, but the inevitable result was that by the First
World War, Britain suddenly realized with a sense of horror that

she was in the grip of a timber famine. A wave of panic swept through Parliament. Politicians began scouring around for somewhere to start planting new trees. Planned forests became the catchword. Planned forests on a hitherto unimagined scale – a new development in agriculture. The pendulum had swung in the opposite direction. Suddenly everyone had become not merely conservation conscious but re-creative too: they wanted to cover the place over with trees, blot out the landscapes in great rolling blankets of foliage, alter the whole face and character of these islands so that never again would Britain find herself in such an embarrassing predicament. It was a splendid idea, at least on paper. The question was – on an already overpopulated island like ours, where could you build forests of such a dimension? The politicians scuttled like beetles from one end of the country to the other, until finally someone came up with the suggestion that the Scottish Border would provide the ideal testing ground for their new tree-planting policies. It was not such a bad choice at that, for at the time the Border was not only one of the least developed and most thinly-peopled areas in Britain, it was also, in agricultural terms, virtually worthless. The land has never been ideal for ploughing. The Ice-Age glaciers left the shales and limestones so deeply buried beneath Boulder Clay that thick beds of peat have developed wherever the drainage was poor. Mosses, rushes, purple moor grass, deer grass and heather cling to the bare hillsides, making them almost useless to all but the hardiest farmer. So to begin with, the politicians saw a vast area of British countryside virtually going begging, nobody using it, nobody wanting it. On top of that, the area was caught in the grip of both a pastoral and an economic slump. Merino wool, imported from abroad had caused a fall in wool prices. Imports in beef and lamb had led to a decline in the price of meat. Hay intakes on the hill farms had dwindled to practically nothing, and disease was running rife among breeding ewes and lambs. There was, in terms of hard cash, nothing whatever to recommend the Border to farmers just after the First World War. It was finished, played out, whacked, kaput. The land was cheap and ready for the taking. The politicians stuck their little flags in the map. The border it would be.

When the Forestry Commission swung into action in the early

twenties, it was able to buy up huge tracts of land at bargain prices. It began with 2000 acres at Smales, not far from Kielder, then bit by bit began adding to them. In 1932 it purchased 47,000 acres from the Duke of Northumberland. The Border Forest was no longer a dream in a politician's briefcase, it was a reality. It existed, the land existed, the trees were being planted with furious rapidity.

Those early days were filled with experiment and hope. The new plantations were laid out on scientific terms. Particular attention was given to the possibility of fire, for no-one wanted to see the meticulous efforts of those post-war years wiped out in one fell swoop through somebody's lack of planning. The trees were laid in compartments of about twentyfive acres each, rimmed with rides and fire breaks. Even the simple and apparently straightforward business of planting went through a series of trials and improvements. In the beginning, the young trees were placed directly into the surface of the peaty soil, but research gradually showed that cutting drainage channels with hand tools, and planting the trees on the resultant turf brought better results.

Slowly, steadily, the forest began to grow. It was soon evident that whereas the original considerations of the politicians had been economic, their choice had been a wise one, for the land was tailor-made for forest development. As far back as 1814 when the historian John Hodgson visited the area, he remarked that the countryside only needed draining and stimulating with lime to make it ideal for the growing of trees. He recorded too how the entire region was infested with insects which bred in the stagnant water of the moors to such a degree that the inhabitants were forced to wear black crepe veils sewn to little skull caps whenever they ventured out of doors.

By the late thirties and early forties, the Border Forest was blooming, but it was still too early to reap its benefits. In any event it was, and still is, too pitifully small to cater for more than minute fragment of the country's needs. When the Second World War came along, Britain's timber shortage was found to be as bad as ever. Once again the politicians turned their eyes northward. The timber famine had given them a fright, and they were filled with the same zeal and enthusiasm their fathers had been. Timber. The country had to have timber. In 1945, Parliament decided it was time to forget half-measures and create five million acres of forest over the next fifty years, some of it by fresh planting, and some of it by the regeneration of natural woodlands.

The Border Forest now swung into top gear. It began to create new plantations and to thin out the old ones. But here the Commission ran into a monumental snag. Choosing the Border as its site had seemed a marvellous idea in 1926, but as the Forest developed, it became painfully clear that more and more people were going to be needed to work it. Where would they come from? There was nowhere – no natural source of human power. The nearest big towns were Newcastle and Berwick. The nearest villages were Wark, Bellingham and Otterburn, and these lay some miles from the Forest itself. Workers had to be transported to and from the plantations, and that cost time and money. The only answer, since the mountain could not come to Mohammed, was to get Mohammed to the mountain. In other words, build a group of settlements, frontier-style, in the very heart of the Forest itself.

Dr Thomas Sharp, a well-known town planning consultant was brought in to sketch out designs for villages which would cater for an entirely new kind of pioneer, a twentieth-century man who demanded more than just the bare necessities of life. He had to design not merely houses, but modern rural communities which would offer up-to-date sanitary arrangements, water and electricity supplies, shops and schools, and facilities for social life as well.

Seven new villages were set up: Kielder, Stonehaugh, Byrness, Kershopefoot, Sleetbeck, Holmfoot and Bonchester Bridge. The workers who came to live in them found sportsfields, social clubs, village halls and playing greens for the children all incorporated into their basic structure. The houses were good: not fancy, but serviceable, and there were facilities too for labourers without families.

They took a bit of getting used to at first. Many of the new Borderers, like my tree-feller in the forest, came from the industrial areas of Tyneside or Central Scotland, and all the social centres in the world could not detract from the overwhelming sense of emptiness and isolation which hangs about the Border fells. Some moved on after only a short stay. But others remained, and bit by bit they settled in. Like the trees themselves, the hillside communities took root and began to grow. At last the lifeline for the Border Forest, the arteries and organs which would supply its needs and make it live had been slowly but firmly established.

I left the forest eventually, not because it ended, but because it divided itself into two, sweeping outwards like an encircling army, leaving a vast stretch of open fellside running up the middle. The going proved tougher here. The ground was soft and littered with peat bogs. Even the tufts of long, coarse grass seemed unstable, as if the earth might tilt beneath me at any moment. I slowed to a crawl, huffing and puffing and oozing with sweat, as I shuffled from hummock to hummock, recalling a friend of mine who used to label them – rather unkindly, I thought – Scotsman's heads. Evening was coming on, and mist hung in the hollows like little blobs of cotton wool. The forest was darkening, the trees losing their density and moulding into a thick black carpet that shuffled inexhaustably on. I had no wish to spend a night among these waterlogged fells, and after studying the map for a few moments, decided to take a chance and strike south through the firebreaks in the hope of reaching the village of Kielder three miles below. It was a decision I came to regret. The breaks, which had looked from a distance as clear as a three-lane motorway, proved to be tangled webs of long grass, shrub and decaying timber. Added to this, the air was literally swarming with millions of insects who honed in on me mercilessly. Every step I took seemed to unearth a fresh brood of buzzing, swirling, zooming tyrants. I swung at them, clawed them off my hair, swatted them with branches, spat at them, swore at them, tried to run away from them, and ended up finally, in spite of the heat, tugging on my anorak and lacing up the hood.

Darkness came creeping in subtly – not falling, as the poets suggest, but rising out of the hollows and folds. The forest began to change. Its contours merged as night came on. Mist curled among its branches, smudging the topmost tips into a bleary haze that seemed to ooze into the sky with no dividing line. I was lost. That awful chilling moment of realization. What a horrible sound that word has. Lost. Short and sweet and to the point, like all words harbouring dire consequences: hurt, break, twist, die. Lost.

Bumpety-bumpety-bumpety-bump, I rattled and clattered and banged my way on. I crossed a river, followed a firebreak that came to a sudden end. How cruel. How unkind. The forest was out to trap me, to circle me, to cheat me, to ensnare me. It would swallow me up like the ravenous monster it was. I was lost.

I turned back, found another fire break and began to stumble along it, thinking dismally of a story I had seen in a newspaper about an unfortunate woman who had wandered into these very trees and whose body had not been discovered till many weeks later. My brain ran on, recalling dreadful episodes in my life. There was a waiter I had known in Vancouver, Canada, who had gone hunting one day and had died after stumbling helplessly about in thick pine trees less than fifty yards from the road.

The sky swirled down to mingle with the treetops. Unseen branches brushed into my face. Pine needles dripped in my hair like pepper grains. I sprawled and fell, clambered up and sprawled again. The ground was a gauntlet of hidden hazards, out to trick me. I stumbled, slurping in the mud. There was no depth or distance, no sense of perspective at all: just a dense wall of shadow that sometimes had substance and sometimes did not.

It looked, I thought miserably, as if I was going to have to spend the night in this insect-ridden fly-swarming strip of muddy eternity. What an infuriating thought. What a dreadful prospect. To lie all night on a soggy mattress of peat, while bugs chewed at my skin.

The trees grew blacker, the air grew thicker, and then, like a hazy patch of mist I spotted a clearing ahead, and beyond it what seemed to my hot and confused little brain the rim of a wooden fence. The forest fences were wire things: a wooden fence had to mean something. A boundary, a garden. The start of human habitation.

I floundered under the trees, struggling across the narrow clearing. It *was* a fence, rough-hewn and with the bark still on it. I followed it along, patting its rail with my left hand. The branches pulled back in front of me like a curtain drawn up on a stage. The sky filtered through, a wide sky, bright and clear and filled with stars. Distant hills leaned high into the moonlight. Below, the forest parted into a broad valley and in its lap, like a childhood dream of fairyland, nestled the twinkling lights of Kielder.

5

Fire Fire

I spent the rest of that night in the official camp-site two miles
down the road. After my mud-and-fly infested scramble in the
firebreaks, it seemed like the Hilton Hotel. The only other
occupants were two families in caravans en route to Scotland.
There was a little camp-site shop, but it was closed by the time I
arrived, and had not opened when I got up next morning, so I
strolled back to Kielder to get a glimpse of the village in
daytime. It was not much to look at. Forestry villages seldom are.
The houses ran in uniform terraces with neat little windows,
front doors, arches, natty little gardens all in a row and all totally
out of context with the landscape around them. With apologies
to designer Dr Sharp, the houses, like the forest, simply do not
belong. They look lost and bewildered, incongrous fragments of
some city council estate in an even more incongruous setting, but
they appeared functional enough, and perhaps for workers fresh
from the towns they brought a little breath of home.

Above them, the forest crouched on the hills like an enemy,
waiting to take over. Wherever you looked, right, left, up,
down, the horizon was bristling with trees. Although the Border
Forest is made up of six smaller forests, North Kielder, Mounces,
Falstone, Tarset, Redesdale and Walk, to all intents and purposes
you can not tell the difference between them and I was, at that
moment, standing at their very heart, almost at the point where
they all began. The first trial planting took place just a few miles
down the valley at Falstone. Nearly 1000 kilometres of new road
have been laid out by the Forestry Commission to make the
plantations accessible, but somehow the overall impression of
Kielder remains one of total isolation. The nearest railway station
is at Hexham on the Newcastle – Carlisle line and that is a good

thirty miles away. A bus service operates from Newcastle to the
village of Bellingham just down the valley, but it is still a fair
haul to Kielder itself, and only infrequent buses penetrate this far
north. There is no hotel accommodation. The nearest licensed
inns are at Falstone and Bellingham, although for those walkers
who do not fancy a night on the camp-site, the village does boast
a youth hostel. But it is not surprising that Kielder manages to
maintain the impression of being a pioneer village tucked into
the folds of the great forest apron.

It is worth mentioning incidentally, if you happen to do the
walk yourself and have an hour or two to spare, that Bellingham
is a good spot to visit. It is only fourteen miles away, and should
your arrival at Kielder correspond with one of the southbound
buses, it would be a shame not to take advantage of it.
Bellingham is not a particularly picturesque village, but it *is* an
interesting one. It has a small spring called Cuddy's well which is
said to have miraculous healing powers. Cuddy presumably was
St Cuthbert, who baptized converts in the spring sometime
around 670 A.D. There is a story that his apparition appeared in
the twelfth century to heal a young girl whose left hand had
twisted into a useless claw. Some of the stones in St Cuthbert's
church date from the twelfth century too, although the building
got so bashed about during the Border raids that little of its
original shape remains. The man responsible for that was Sir
Walter Scott of Buccleuch, the same Buccleuch who broke
Kinmont Willie out of Carlisle Castle. He gave Bellingham a
hammering in July 1597 when he crossed the Border with 400
men, stole the cattle from the surrounding fields and turned his
guns on the church. Three small cannon balls were found during
alterations on the roof in 1861, and they can be seen inside the
building today.

Buccleuch seems to have had a private fixation about
Bellingham, for the village became one of his favourite targets.
Mind you, he did not get things all his own way. During one of
the Northumbrian retaliatory raids north, the sword of
Buccleuch's grandfather was captured by the Charlton family.
Buccleuch was apparently very fond of the sword which he
regarded as a family heirloom. He protested to Cardinal Wolsey
who is said to have ordered the Charltons to give it back. Their

reply was a defiant: "If he wants it, he must come and take it". Buccleuch never did. The sword still lies preserved at nearby Hesleyside alongside the famous Charlton spur which, according to Border custom, used to be served at dinner as a gentle hint to the men of the house that the lady was running short of housekeeping money.

The tombstones in Bellingham's churchyard are fascinating to walk among. Some of them are so old that their inscriptions are barely readable, but the most interesting of all is a stone which bears no name or mark whatsoever. It is shaped like a pack or haversack, and its surface has been pounded smooth by centuries of wind and weather. The man beneath it has never been identified. He met his death in a particularly bizarre way. It was in winter 1723, when a pedlar called at nearby Lee Hall and left his bag with the servants of the house while he went to look for lodgings for the night. The man promised to return for it as soon as he found a suitable inn or boarding house and the servants left it on the kitchen hearth. But while they were preparing the evening meal, one of them noticed that the bag had moved. He seized an old blunderbuss and fired pointblank into its canvas casing. The pack was opened, and inside the servants found the body of a young man with a whistle tied around his neck.

Now even as late as the eighteenth century, life on the Border could be a fairly hazardous business, and there was no doubt in anyone's mind that the young man had been deliberately planted in the household, either to burgle it or to act as the spearhead of a larger force. That night, a contingent of local farmhands armed themselves with shotguns and stationed themselves at the windows of the darkened hall. Just before twelve, they heard a long low call from behind the shadowy clumps of shrubbery. One of the farmhands took the whistle from the dead man's neck and blew it softly in reply. There was a moment of silence, then from the darkness a band of horsemen came galloping into the courtyard. The farmhands did not bother to challenge them, they simply opened fire. Cut to ribbons, the intruders were forced to retreat, but they dragged their dead and injured with them and succeeded in making a clean escape. In the days that followed, a vigorous search was conducted throughout the surrounding countryside, but no trace of the invaders' identity or whereabouts was ever discovered. The young man who had been shot, was buried in Bellingham churchyard, and his tombstone – a rather fitting one – was fashioned in the shape of a pedlar's pack.

But coming back to Kielder, it took me less than five minutes to wander through the village from end to end. There were no shops apart from the post office, which does sell minor items of food like cakes, sweets and lemonade. At the top of the street however, the mobile grocery van was doing a brisk trade and I joined the queue, hoping to pick up a few tins of meat and vegetables. I stood chatting to a woman in a bright lemon headscarf who told me she had come from Teeside, where her husband had worked in the huge I.C.I. chemical works four years before. Like my man in the forest, she too was happy at having made the switch.

"The trouble with city life," she said, "is that everybody's moving too fast. They don't have time to stop, or even talk. Out here, it's a different world. There isn't a man, woman or child in this village I don't know. You feel part of a great big family."

"What about tourists?" I asked.

"Well, we get one or two," she said, "Not enough to intrude."

She sniffed and added: "That'll change soon enough though. They're flooding the valley to the south to make a new reservoir, which means they'll be building a new road through here and opening the area up. There'll be sailing and fishing and God knows what else. Come back in five years' time and I'll bet you won't even recognize the place."

I had already heard about the reservoir scheme which, like most reservoir schemes had sparked off its share of controversy. Flooding Kielder Valley means wiping out good farmland for one thing, to say nothing of the trees which have been planted there. There have been objections from people whose livelihood will be affected and from naturalists and botonists who feel that animal and plant life will be wiped out. On top of that, as the lady said, a new reservoir means new roads and new roads mean tourists. Lots of tourists. They will come in at weekends from Tyneside and Teeside, Carlisle and Berwick, choking the highways, flooding the tiny villages. With the hillsides all forested where else can they go? Kielder is unlikely to retain its sense of isolation very much longer.

Already, the Forestry Commission is laying its plans for the expected invasion. Nature trails are being set up with signposted routes and lettered posts marking items of special interest. Observation hides are being built to enable visitors to photograph wild life. Picnic sites are being created, with log seats, toilets and car parks. An information centre has been established at nearby Kielder Castle, and a Forest Park Museum at the entrance to the camp site. There is even a scenic Forest Drive where, for thirty pence, you can chug in your car along twelve miles of panoramic views of farm, forest and moorland. In Kielder today it is all systems go. The village is poised and ready for its tourist industry to begin. All it needs is a means of getting them there, and once the reservoir road is built, the flood gates will be well and truly open.

I paused for a few minutes on the village outskirts to look at the old Kielder Viaduct. I love those old-fashioned railway bridges, particularly when you see them in wild open country. The arches blend in so well with the sweep and curl of fell and hillside. They make some of the more modern constructions look a bit soulless by comparison.

Kielder Viaduct was built in 1862 to carry the Redesmouth to Riccarton line. The line has been closed for years now, but the viaduct still stands, and it is a fine example of old railway architecture.

I do not suppose anyone would say that Kielder Castle is a fine example of anything. It is not even a real castle. But it makes a marvellous sight when you first set eyes on it, nestling in among the trees. Half-close your eyes and you might be staring at one of Ludwig of Bavaria's creations. Or even the hunting lodge from the Prisoner of Zenda. In fact, a hunting lodge is precisely what it is. Or was. It was built by the Duke of Northumberland in 1775, and Sir Walter Scott in his *Journal* dated October 7th, 1827 says:

The Duke tells me his people in Keeldar were all quite wild the first time his father went up to shoot there. The women had no other dress than a bedgown and petticoat. The men were savage and could hardly be brought to rise from the heath, either from sulleness or fear. They sung a wild tune the burden of which was "Ourina Ourina Ourina". The females sung, the men danced round and at a certain part of the tune they drew their dirks which they always wore.

Today though, the castle houses the headquarters of the Forestry Commission. It is one of the few pieces of Kielder which clicks into place with the countryside around it. The grey stone walls, the little turrets look perfectly at home in the rolling sea of spruce and pine.

I had arranged to meet our film crew here at half-past ten, for we were due to film our most spectacular event of the week, a forest fire, lit specially for us under the wary eyes of the forest fire-fighting team. I peered at my watch. Barely nine-thirty. I had more than an hour to wait.

There was a tiny cafe tucked around the side of the castle car park and I waded my way through a breakfast of eggs, bacon, sausage and fried bread, then wandered round to the front entrance to see what I could discover about the forest itself.

A very pretty girl showed me into an office overlooking the car park. The walls were lined with maps covering the vast areas already planted, with shaded bits indicating the sections due for expansion or thinning out. A tin of nescafé stood on the filing cabinet, and there were all the usual bits and pieces you expect to find in Ministry buildings. The forest officer himself was a pleasant man with a nice sense of humour who would have looked more at home, I thought, sitting in the office of a country lawyer or doctor. We drank instant coffee out of big white mugs and he lit his pipe while I told him how I felt about the way the Forestry Commission went on systematically wiping out the hillsides. His eyes twinkled.

"You're being very unfair, you know," he said, "Forests don't destroy land, they preserve it. Do you know what is happening to the topsoil all over the world at this moment? It's being steadily demolished. Bit by bit, its' blowing away. Do you realize the time will come — not in our life, thank God — when there will be no more arable topsoil left, and then what will the human race do? Nothing will grow, because there will be nothing to grow *on*, and the earth will be turned into a total desert — a dead planet, in fact, like the moon. Now forests can't stop that sort of thing, but they can slow down the process. They control the erosion of the soil, you see. The canopy of trees breaks the force of violent winds and rain. The tree roots help to hold the earth in place. The twigs which decay make the ground more porous and a more effective reservoir for the storage of water. They also moderate the air temperature, keep the local climate steady, help crop production in farmland nearby and protect natural watersheds. It's easy to moan that they get in your way, but without them we'd be in a very sorry state indeed."

I sat looking at him, feeling like an idiot. It hadn't occurred to me that way.

"What about wild life?" I protested, "When you plough up hillsides, fence off open land, you must destroy the breeding grounds of thousands of birds and animals."

He chuckled.

"That's absolute nonsense," he said, "Forests revive wild life, they don't destroy it. At the turn of the century, the roe deer was practically extinct in these hills. Now you'll find them all over the place. We've got mountain hare and red squirrels, foxes, badgers, otters, wild goats, red grouse and blackcock, buzzards, merlins, hawks and kestrels. The forest is a teeming bed of wild life."

I sat for a moment, thinking that over.

"Well," I said, "It's not going to last much longer, is it?"

"How d'you mean?"

"When the new reservoir is built, you'll be swamped with tourists, for one thing."

He shook his head.

"I don't see that that'll make much difference. It's hardly likely to affect the wild life which tends to stick to the more inaccessible areas anyway."

"But it's going to change the nature of things, isn't it? It must do. You can't expect people to be herded around like cattle."

He smiled.

"We like to pride ourselves on planning ahead as far as we can. We've been laying out forest trails and picnic sites and goodness knows what else. When the visitors come, we'll be ready for them."

"Won't they offer a serious fire hazard? I imagine with all the timber you've got here, the slightest mistake could set off the lot like a tinder box?"

He scratched his nose thoughtfully with his pipe stem.

"We do try to make visitors aware of the dangers," he said, "and as a rule they act quite responsibly. You have to remember that it's a very moist climate we have in this country. We're not up against the same degree of fire hazard as say Canada or the United States. We have our bad times of course. Early spring's the worst, when the bracken and undergrowth is brittle and dry. That's the real danger period. Cigarette ends, matches, even fragments of glass left lying in the sun are all likely to start the heather smouldering. And when the winds are strong, the flames spread like an express train."

"Does that happen often?" I asked.

"No," he smiled, "Not often. We had a good many fires before they closed the old railway line. The sparks from the locomotives were a continual headache. But these days when a Fire breaks out, it's generally through thoughtlessness: either on the part of visitors, or even one of our own people."

"How do you guard against it ... " I wondered.

"You'll see for yourself," he said, "We've cordoned off a small section of woodland which we plan to set on fire when your film crew arrives. Then we'll go through the process of putting it out."

He waved at a pile of reports on his desk.

"Give me a chance to get some of this paperwork out of the way, and I'll take you up there," he added.

I went outside and wandered around the car park for half an hour. The sky was overcast, a great blanket of surly cloud through which, in places, the sun had somehow managed to nuzzle its way, making the air hot and muggy and filled with the smell of rising sap and hot summer dust. I sat in the car park enjoying the views over spruce-shrouded hills. I tried to imagine them before the forest existed. It was not easy. It seemed so huge, that forest, so peaceful too. Empty, quiet, green and still. And yet, of course, unseen by me, it would be bustling with life. There would be badgers in there, weasels, deer, otter, stoats, foxes, rabbits and hares and goodness knew what else. It was a living forest, and although man had created it, somehow you felt that man only continued to exist there by the good graces of the forest itself.

The film crew turned up twenty minutes late. The forest officer came out to collect me and off we set in convoy, the officer and myself leading the way in his landrover, the others trailing behind in dribs and drabs, bumping, lurching and hiccuping along twisting unpaved roads which sliced deeper and deeper into the hills. On the way, the officer began to explain how the forest operated. The planting of new land goes on continually at the rate of many hundreds of acres each year. And that is in addition to the replanting of areas which have already been felled. So in effect, it is constantly rebuilding itself, shedding off the old, putting on the new.

The laying of fresh plantations is a complicated business. Each year, the forest staff prepare a plan showing where the new roads will run, where the drainage ditches will be dug, where the streams and main water supplies will lie. Then they sketch out the forest compartments, fencing them round with rides and firebreaks. Once the plan has been approved, the hard physical work gets under way. The hillsides have first to be ploughed up, and that is not easy when the land has lain dormant for centuries. Buried boulders can damage cutting blades, and even the peat itself can be coarse and unyielding. A huge hill drainage plough is used, pulled by a powerful crawler tractor. It rips out furrows about five feet apart, and lays down long strips of turf on which the planting will later take place.

After the ploughing, the plantations are fenced off with wide-mesh sheep netting, then the young trees are brought in from the Forestry nurseries, sometimes at the rate of a million a year. By the time they arrive, they are already between eighteen months and four years old, with bushy root systems which give them a good start on the exposed hillsides.

Each member of the planting gang carries a bag filled with young trees slung around his shoulder, and a long-handled spade. He cuts a slit through the turf and lays in the tree roots, planting them carefully about five feet apart. The process is carried out at great speed. One man will lay between 1000 and 1500 new trees every day, and almost every one will take root.

For the first year or two they have to be tended constantly, and the grass and bracken which spring up around them cut with a reaping hook in summer. After that however, the trees need little help from the forester, and so long as the plantations are securely fenced off against sheep, deer, hares and wild goats, they will continue to grow happily until the time comes for thinning out.

The biggest single danger is the forest officer's worst nightmare: fire. Alongside the main roads, sheep and cattle are used to keep the herbage short, rendering it less likely to ignite. At intervals too along the roadside, stacks of fire brooms have been established ready for beaters to go into action at first sight of flame or smoke.

As we jostled our way higher and higher, I spotted the slender framework of a metal lookout tower perched on a nearby hilltop.

"How many of those do you have?" I asked.

"Only four in this area," the forest officer said, "But they're enough. We keep them constantly manned during the high-risk periods, and the watchers are linked by telephone to the fire control centre. As soon as a watcher spots a suspicious spiral of smoke, the man at the centre can find out its exact location by getting a cross-bearing from another tower."

I peered at the flimsy metal framework. It looked like a derelict rocket launching pad. I remembered years earlier, standing in the press box at Cape Kennedy, watching an Apollo missile about to thrust itself into space. The tower, with its snub nose and lean flanks reminded me of that, or rather of its skeleton, thin and brittle and ready to snap.

"How high would you say it was?" I murmured.

"Couple of hundred feet or so."

I peered dubiously at the narrow struts.

"Looks as if a strong puff of wind would blow it over," I grunted.

"I doubt it," he chuckled, "It's been in these hills a damn sight longer than I have and I imagine it'll still be here after I've gone. Take a look, if you like. You get a spectacular view from the top."

He pulled the landrover to a halt, a tricky little smile playing around the corners of his mouth. He thinks I am scared, I thought. I clambered out and strolled up the hill to where the tower stood tall and solitary. It looked as if it had been built with a child's meccano set. The ladder felt even flimsier than the girders, and as I mounted, it began to shiver beneath me, as if the whole contraption was on the point of crashing around my ears. I climbed higher, a soft wind ruffling my hair. I kept my eyes fixed on the rung ahead, moving up one rung at a time, trying to look neither up nor down, knowing instinctively that the forest officer was watching from below with that amused glint in his eye.

I reached the tiny matchbox cabin. My God, was I that high already? Wind scoured my cheeks. My fingers felt chill against the cold hard metal. I pushed open the trapdoor, got my arms inside and hauled myself up. It was empty. And small. Incredibly small. How could you move in such a place? I thought. I felt that if I took a really deep breath I would fill the cabin from corner to corner.

I let the trapdoor flop with a soft thud and peered through the windows at the vast sweeps of forest dipping away on every side. Wherever I looked, there were trees. I felt as if the entire world was covered with trees. Big trees, small trees, fat trees, thin trees, tall trees, short trees, leafy trees, bare trees, spiky trees, smooth trees. Trees everywhere. Up and downhill they marched in neatly-regimented rows.

To the north, I could see the castle. Barely the size of a postage stamp, it looked, in the endless foliage, like a liferaft on a dark stormy ocean.

I came down eventually with some sense of relief, and we drove on along the winding rolling track.

"What do you do when a fire's spotted?" I asked.

"Call the fire brigade," he answered shortly.

I looked at him.

"But that's in Bellingham, fourteen miles away."

"Well, we've got our own fire-fighting unit to hold the flames in check till they get here. Our men use specially equipped landrovers and lorries. We've got a short-wave radio installation to enable the fire control centre to keep in touch with watchtowers and vehicles, and if things get really out of hand we can even call in troops. Most of the time though, we manage to get the flames out before reinforcements are needed."

We rounded a corner and the trees seemed to fall away, leaving a wide area of open moorland with a phalanx of forest trickling across it. This was to be the site of our fire. A small knot of men stood around in the heather: they were there to ensure that the flames did not get beyond their allocated section. As we slithered to a halt, I noticed with a sense of surprise that smoke was already rising from a clump of tufty brown grass.

"Call that a fire?" I said, disappointed, "It's not even big enough to boil a kettle."

He laughed.

"That's how they nearly all start," he said, "Watch how fast it spreads."

The smoke billowed and swelled, growing thicker and stronger by the second. Whiffs of it drifted past my nostrils, pungent and prickly. Our camera crew were out of their car and racing about, shooting everything in sight. In the heather, the knot of men stood staring at it all impassively.

I fixed my eyes on the column of smoke, watching fascinated as it twisted and twirled, wriggled and slithered, rising, always rising, up, up and away. Soon I could see flames licking into the sky. Still no-one made a move to put it out.

"What happens now?" I murmured.

The forest officer settled himself comfortably into his seat and began to re-fill his pipe.

"By now the smoke should have been spotted," he said, "The call will have gone through to Bellingham, and our own unit will be on its way here. Whether they arrive in time to put out the flames on their own we'll just have to wait and see."

Smoke drifted across the windscreen, bringing with it the harsh scent of burning vegetation. Sparks danced into the air, crackling loudly like a million jumping jacks going off at once, A huge glob of blackened earth appeared in the middle of the heather. Black fumes tinged with crimson flung themselves skyward. Within seconds, the fire was among the trees, leaping between their trunks like a frenzied animal, growling, growing, expanding, multiplying with terrifying ferocity. What had been, just a moment before, a lazy smudge of moor smoke had turned in a twinkling into an inferno.

"Now it's really got its teeth in," the forest officer declared mildly, "Best we can hope for is to stop it spreading till the brigade gets here."

I stared in awe as the flames licked their way up each

individual trunk, crawling higher and higher, growing stronger with every inch. Fire billowed between the roots, setting the trees in stark relief, pointing them up as they crackled their lives out in cascading sparks. Still the watchers stood grimly by. We have gone too far, I thought. They will never put it out now. It will spread. It will go through the forest like an angel of death. The whole plantation will be reduced to ashes.

With a roar of discovery, the flames found a fresh trunk, then another, gobbling them up with furious voracity. Crack, crack, crackle, crackle, the flames bit, the trees blazed, the skyline turned into a solid wall of flame.

Around our heads, the air seemed to lurch as oxygen was sucked into the maelstrom. I heard the clatter of a truck engine as the fire unit went racing by my window. Smoothly and efficiently they went to work, rolling out lengths of hose and sinking the ends into one of the strategic waterholes which have been dug every four hundred yards throughout the forest.

"What are they playing at?" I growled, "They're laying the hose *behind* the flames."

The forest officer winked.

"You'll see in a moment," he promised.

They started the pump, and dancing fountains of water sprinkled out along the hoses' entire length. The canvas had been peppered with small holes, creating a shield of solid water which held the flames back and prevented them spreading to other parts of the forest.

"That's what we call the Holy Hose," the forest officer said with a grin.

From somewhere far back, came the distant clanging of bells. The sound grew louder, swelling in volume, blotting out the crackle of blazing timber, becoming constant, insistent, and as I peered through the rear window I saw the unlikely picture of three fire engines lurching at top speed up the bumpy forest track.

"The cavalry to the rescue," I murmured.

Out they leapt, their helmets and belt buckles brightly gleaming. Within a minute, the whole area was a scene of stampeding action. Firemen raced up and down, bellowing orders. Hoses unrolled. Water squirted. Cameras whirred. Great colums of spray leapt into the air like searchlight beams. Gracefully, they curled into the very heart of the fire and the timber hissed in huge clouds of escaping steam. By now, the flames had been safely cordoned off by the Holy Hose, and within minutes, in spite of its ferocity, the blaze had been brought under control. I breathed a sigh of relief. For a dreadful moment, I had been afraid that we had overplayed our hands. I saw in my mind four hundred square miles of blazing timber and the awful task of trying to explain it to the BBC Expenses Department.

Now only the blackened treestumps remained to testify that the fire had ever existed.

"Thank God," I breathed.

The fire officer seemed amused.

"That was nothing," he said, "A little exercise, no more."

"For a minute or two," I said, "I thought it was out of control."

He laughed.

"Not a chance," he said, "Forestry fire protection costs the taxpayer more than £300,000 a year. It's not just good, it's the best. Thirty years ago we lost nearly a thousand acres in only a few hours. We make damned sure nowadays that never happens again."

He turned the starter, revving the engine back into life.

"All this excitement's given me an appetite," he said, "Let's go back to the castle and get some lunch."

6

Swains, Scoundrels and Scribblers

A few miles north of Kielder, the Border traces the feathery line of a narrow burn before careering off across Peel Fell. I had said goodbye to my forest officer, and to the film crew, and with a stomach full of fish fingers and chips set off up the dour spruce-flanked hump which would lead eventually to the Border ridge. It felt good to be on the move once more, to listen to the chomp-chomp-chomp of my boots on the earth and feel that satisfying glow as my body moved into its second wind. Around me, the nature of the landscape was changing yet again. I was leaving the forest behind. It fell away in dribs and drabs until after an hour or two, only a few hardy clusters of Scots pine remained, clinging to the bare hillsides like incongruous tufts of hair.

By now, my left boot was beginning to act up again. I could feel the nails pricking into the soft underpadding of my big toe. The going was unpleasant in the extreme. The grass clumps got clumpier, the peat bogs got boggier, and on top of it all, mist came drifting around my cheeks like strands of fleecy cotton wool. The land seemed as if it had been painted against a slate grey sky, drained of colour, without relief from the monotonous sweep of heather and peat.

I sank up to my knees in slime. Sweat oozed from my pores in a steady stream. I thought I had never seen a more inhospitable landscape in my life. There was simply no break at all: no farms, no roads, no trees, no fields. Not even sheep. Just mile after mile of bleak hills and even bleaker sky.

As I climbed higher, the mist began to thicken, and soon visibility had been cut to no more than fifteen or twenty feet. I could feel its damp touch on my throat, its moisture beading my hair. It seemed to curl out of the ground itself, swirling around my feet as if I had somehow been transported back in time to an earth still cooling and devoid of life.

With the mist, the density seemed drained from the air, so that only my huffing and puffing told me whether I was going up or down. Gullies lay like simple patterns on a flat unending landscape. Hilltops were darker patches on an ocean of coaly grey. It would not have surprised me greatly to have seen Frankenstein's monster lurching out of the fog, for strange shapes were springing up all over the place with terrifying suddenness: boulders, peat-furrows, glistening outcrops of jagged rock.

I dug out my map and took a compass bearing. There were no landmarks to speak of, nothing at all of substance to work from, but the needle kept me going east. As I climbed higher, the ground became honeycombed with massive gullies of wet peat, and I found myself having again and again to retrace my steps, or wade thigh and knee deep through treacly goo. I gained height and the wind picked up, pummelling my face and chest in a series of combination punches that took my breath away. Maybe, I thought, I was on the rim of hell itself. That is what it seemed like. Strange how one's fancy runs riot in wild surroundings. Small wonder that the Border is riddled with legend. This landscape had the stuff of superstition in it. Satan might be swaying happily in that drifting mist. Hobgoblins might be lurking in the gullies of spongy mud. The real world – if there was a real world left – seemed a thousand miles away.

I looked at my watch. Early evening. The prospect of a night on such dreary fells was a far from pleasant one and I tried to quicken my pace, scrambling from fissure to fissure like a man demented. Suddenly, out of the heather, a moorhen flung herself into the air in a great squall of shrieks and flapping wings. In front of my feet, half-a-dozen furry chicks ran squeaking into the cover of the long grass. I moved more slowly after that, taking care where I thumped my boots. The sight of that little furry family had cheered me immensely. At least, I thought, I was not the *only* living thing in this nightmare.

The ground steepened again, and as I climbed higher, something strange began to happen. The mist grew pale, and through it penetrated a sense of muggy warmth. It was like moving into a stream of hot water in a chilly swimming pool.

The peat gullies grew fewer, and as I climbed, boulders swayed into my path, gained solidity, became rough or smooth, easy to spot, and I knew the mist was thinning out. Then, with a suddenness that was breathstopping, I was all at once above it. Just like that. One second the world was a blanket of suffocating grey, the next I was perched on the hillside with a great ocean of bubbly white cloud below me. What a sight. It licked at the shores of my solitary island like a sea of fleece. I cursed myself for not having a camera to record it. It was one of those things you see no more than once or twice in a lifetime and which you can never re-create. Ahead, the ridge rippled east, climbing out of the cloud like a mystic stairway to heaven. The sky was stunningly blue and the sun, even at that time of evening, was warm enough for me to take off my anorak and tuck it under the haversack strap.

I set off along the spine of my island, glad to be out in the sunwarmed air, feeling as if I had somehow climbed to the topmost tip of the world. There was nothing to see but the ridge in front, the cloud below, the sky above. No other hilltop pierced the surface of that fluffy ocean. For a moment I caught a glimpse of a shallow valley just to the south, but even as I watched, cloud oozed into it like melting ice cream. What a country, I thought jubilantly, forgetting, now that I had the sun to cheer me, how austere and menacing it had seemed only a minute or two before.

Another hour, and the cloud began to part like the ocean under Moses's rod. The shadows were lengthening, casting deep lines below the outcrops of rock and throwing the ridge ahead into sharp relief. Two narrow strips of spruce were stuck on the hillside like band-aids, and a solitary tractor chugged peacefully away on its lower flanks. Ahead, the land seemed to surge suddenly into a series of angry fluctuating breakers and with a sense of joy I recognized the familiar russet hummocks of the Cheviot Hills. My own Cheviots. Hills I had wandered since boyhood. I was home.

The hillside suddenly tumbled into a steep grassy pass, and there I spotted Carter Bar, the steepest, the wildest and the most breathtaking highway linking Scotland and England. It curls its way over the hilltops like a frozen glacier, going nowhere it seems, lost, aimless, a ribbon of concrete wriggling in and out between the summits, tracing an indeterminate line that looks as if the slightest snowstorm would choke it to a standstill: which of course is precisely what happens nearly every winter. And yet it was along this road that the famous Newcastle–Edinburgh coach *The Chevy Chase* used to trundle its way in the early 1800s. When you look at the ruggedness of that country, at the sheer loneliness and isolation of the terrain, it seems a remarkable feat for a passenger service to achieve. The horses must have been titans to take that gradient, or perhaps in those days the riders got out and walked up the steep bits. I know this much: between November and March, the vehicles were repeatedly bogged down in drifting snow, and still the coach line went on operating. Do not forget there were no heating facilities then. You took a blanket and a muffler, and if you were lucky you got to the other end without pneumonia.

Once, making a film, I had to ride in a coach across Morecambe Bay. The wind was blowing up and the buggy seemed so brittle, so light and dainty and ready to crumple into bits under the shuddering gusts that I rode with the door handle already turned in case I had to jump for it. I tried to imagine traversing Carter Bar in midwinter in a thing like that. It seemed a suicidal notion, but I suppose people were tougher then. Or else they were less conscious or concerned with physical comforts. In any event, the newspaper advertisements of the day offered a service "fitted with spring cushions inside and driven by one coachman in thirteen hours through the beautifully picturesque scenery on the road by Otterburn, Jedburgh, Melrose, Galashiels to Edinburgh, arriving at nine o'clock in time for the Mail to Glasgow." The fare was twenty-eight shillings if you rode inside, and fifteen shillings if you rode outside.

Ten years later, the owners of *The Chevy Chase* were boasting that they had cut its travelling time from thirteen hours to eleven-and-a-half hours, but by then the sands were running out for the old coaching firms. The face of Britain was being changed by a new monster, one which needed no horses to pull it and which ran on glistening roadways of steel. The linking of the English and Scottish railways at Berwick marked the end of the coach line. The primitive journey across Carter Bar was no longer necessary. The train was faster, cheaper and infinitely safer. Would-be travellers switched to rail and by the mid-1840s the coach service had sunk into obscurity. It seems a shame somehow, the end of an era. Progress is inevitable, I suppose, but it often tends to destroy things which are precious or colourful. I can never look at Carter Bar without getting a mental picture of a flimsy carriage battling its way through a snowy winter's night, horses straining, hides and nostrils steaming, passengers and coachmen shivering in tundra vistas of snow and ice.

I found a brook running below the highway and put up my tent beside a battered copse of ancient trees. I was hungry again, but the thought of heating up something to eat seemed too much trouble, so I opened a can of beer and began to spread peanut butter on chunks of slightly soggy french bread. Darkness was falling fast, and already the nearby copse of trees had merged into a sliver of shade on the mottled hill. The brook twisted away below me, following the incline of the valley floor, and just below my camp-site I could see the bobbing line of Batinghope burn, a barely distinguishable gash in the grass-cluttered peat. I shuffled around and faced the other way while I went on making my peanut-butter sandwiches. I did not like to look at Batinghope burn with darkness coming on for it had a grisly story behind it, that one, a story to make you think of ghosts and ghoulies and other supernatural things, particularly with the sky thickening into a moonless starless void. Parcy Reed was the hero of the tale and he came to a particularly nasty end just a few hundred feet from where I was sitting. Parcy was keeper of Redesdale in the sixteenth century and he had been having trouble with his neighbours, the Crosiers. No-one seems to know what the feud was about, but one day Parcy went hunting with three members of the Hall family, whom he took to be his friends. They wandered rather far from home and decided to spend the night in a wooden hut on Batinghope's bank. When Parcy was asleep, the Halls jammed his sword tight in its scabbard, watered his gunpowder and signalled to the waiting Crosiers to move in for the kill. The Crosier vengeance was a bloody affair in true Border style. They literally chopped Parcy up into little pieces. First, they hacked off his hands and feet and they went on hacking until the fragments of his body had to be collected in pillowcases to be transported home.

I shuddered just thinking about it, and sipped tiredly at my can of beer. Above my head, the little ribbon of toy vehicles went slithering by at a snail's pace. Night closed in as I chewed my peanut-butter sandwiches and the car headlamps made flickering patterns on the hillside. It seemed the end of an eventful day. Forest fires and hill fog, what a combination. I felt drained, worn out – and yet, in terms of actual walking, I had covered barely twelve miles. Have to do better than that, I thought. Tomorrow I would put a spurt on, and with that prophecy, I washed my things in the stream and crawled into bed.

I lay for a while— almost too weary to sleep, thinking in spite of myself of Parcy Reed's extremities littering the grassy bluffs of Batinghope. It can be a bad place to sleep, they say, Carter Bar by night. You hear the screams of the men who have died there in the heather. I am relieved to record that the only thing I heard was the rumble of the trucks and the flapping of my tent roof in the wind.

Next morning, I made my first detour from the Border to visit the ruins of Hermitage Castle, named by one historian "the guardhouse of the bloodiest valley in Britain". If you are walking the Border yourself, then do not miss it: it is well worth taking time out to look at. No fairy-tale castle, this: my God, no. Gaunt and stark, grim and cheerless, it rears up from the hillside like a spectral skeleton. It stands on a bluff overlooking a small level plain on the north bank of Hermitage Water, flanked to the east and west by two small streams, Castle Sike and Lady's Sike, both of which have been used at some time in the past to construct enclosures around the fortifications. The main entrance faces south, and inside, the small central courtyard is typical of fortified manor houses or pele towers found all over the north. Built somewhere around the end of the thirteenth century, it got its name from the ruins of monastic buildings found just west of the walls themselves, for the site was originally a hermitage for monks from Kelso.

Hermitage was the most renowned stronghold on the frontier, the cork that plugged up the whole Liddesdale Valley. It survived century after century of bloodshed, but more than that, it reeks of the very essence of the Border. Harsh, bleak and uncompromising, Hermitage looks exactly as it *should* look, and the dark passions unleashed within and around its walls make Macbeth sound like an amiable country vicar.

The earliest holders were the Soulises, and a fat prize it must have seemed in those days, for whoever controlled the castle controlled the lives of every man, woman and child in Liddesdale, a fact of which Lord William Soulis took full advantage. He sounds a nasty piece of work, forcing the people to live and work like animals, murdering the neighbouring chieftains after inviting them to the castle under the guise of friendship, enticing the famous Tyneside Baron, the Count of Kielder to a grand hunt followed by a banquet, then ordering him to be held under the castle stream until he drowned. He is also renowned for having bartered his soul to the devil – another variation on the Faust theme. The chamber in which the two are said to have conferred is supposed to still exist somewhere beneath the ruins. According to legend, it is opened every seven years by the devil himself, to whom Soulis threw the key when he was leaving home for the final time.

As in all good stories, Soulis got his just desserts. His wickedness eventually so angered the Scottish King that he exclaimed: "Boil him and sup his broo", and his retainers needed no second telling. They wrapped Soulis in a sheet of lead, carried him to an old druid circle a mile north of the castle and boiled him to death in a massive cauldron.

> They rolled him up in a sheet of lead,
> A sheet of lead for a funeral pall;
> They plunged him in the cauldron red,
> And melted him – lead, bones and all.

From the Soulises, the castle passed into the hands of the Douglases who seem to have been intent on even greater acts of infamy. When one of Sir William Douglas's former friends, Sir Alexander Ramsay was appointed Sheriff over Teviotdale, Douglas was so consumed with jealousy that he threw the unfortunate Ramsay and his horse into a dungeon at Hermitage and deliberately starved them to death. If you climb to the first floor of the north-east tower, you will find a spot where a trap door dropped into a deep dark pit. It is lightless, airless, without latrines or sanitation of any kind, and it is here that Ramsay is believed to have been kept. Toward the end of the eighteenth century bits of a bridle and saddle, and the bones of a man and horse were discovered during alterations. It is said that Ramsay managed to cling to life longer than Douglas had anticipated, because he was able to nibble at corn ears which trickled through a crevasse from the granary directly overhead.

The Douglases eventually lost the castle, not through any act of war but because of an outburst of temper on the part of one of their younger members, the Earl of Angus. He was a fiery fellow Angus, as many of the old time Borderers were, and he had been insulted in court by a cavalier called Spens of Kilspindie. Duelling in court was forbidden in those days, for in spite of their brutality, members of both the English and Scottish aristocracy liked to think of themselves as sophisticated and civilized. Angus, however, was not a man to forget an insult, and one day, while hawking near Borthwick, he ran into Spens of Kilspindie quite by accident. He called upon the courtier to answer for his taunts and the two men fought it out with broadswords on the spot. They had little of the style and grace of the classic French duellists, those old swordfights: they were simply brawls, depending more on brute strength than science or skill. Angus, with a single blow, lopped off one of his opponent's legs like a chunk of cucumber, and promptly rode off, leaving Spens to bleed to death in the grass. The result was that the King, angered that two of his courtiers should settle their differences in such a barbaric fashion, forced the Douglases to exchange their lands and castle for those of the Bothwells of Clydesdale.

But murder and violent death go well with Hermitage. It is such a sombre place, so wind-battered, rainwashed, and so curiously spine-chilling. No wonder this castle, which survived centuries of rampage and turmoil, has had a thousand stories told and re-told about it. I must mention one more. It is the most famous story of all. It involves the Earl of Bothwell, that celebrated rascal so beloved by writers of romantic fiction, who was Lieutenant of the Marches of Scotland, Keeper of Liddesdale and holder of the fort of Hermitage in the year 1566. That October, Bothwell set out with his troopers to capture a band of

raiders, led by a notorious freebooter called Jock Elliott of the
Park. The expedition began successfully enough. Bothwell did
take a number of the ruffians prisoner and sent them back to the
castle under heavy guard. But when he caught up with Elliott
himself, Bothwell almost lost his life. He shot Elliott in the thigh,
and believing him dead, or at the very least severely wounded,
he strode up to the fallen outlaw to carry out the *coup de grace*.
Elliott, still very much alive, drew his dagger, pounced upon
Bothwell and managed to stab him three times. The Earl,
desperately injured, was carried back to Hermitage, and it was
here that he received a visit from his lady love, Mary, Queen of
Scots.

Hearing of his condition, the young Queen had ridden all the
way from Jedburgh: she did the journey in one day, twenty-five
miles there, twenty-five miles back, over bog and moorland,
through wind, fog, bitter cold and driving rain. It was no picnic
for a young woman who had never enjoyed the best of health.
According to historians of the time: "She rode with indecent
haste and lowped into bed beside Bothwell". But as one man
who had done the same ride himself told me: "After twenty five
miles across that lot, I didn't feel like lowping into bed with
anybody, and I'm damn sure Mary didn't either".

It was a ride that almost cost her reputation and her life too, for
soon afterwards she contracted a fever and nearly died. So close
was she to the end that they opened the windows to let her spirit
out, and the fresh air appears to have revived her. Years later,
when she was incarcerated at Fotheringay Castle, Mary uttered
what are said to have been the saddest words in Scottish history:
"Would that I had died at Jedburgh".

I spent more than an hour wandering around the ruins of the
castle. I would like to have climbed to the parapet and looked at
the view of the surrounding hills, but the staircases have either
been destroyed or are too worn to be used by the general public.
In any event, a stroll around Hermitage is not a heartwarming
experience. Somehow, the very hardness of its stone walls gives
the place an atmosphere of austerity and malice. And yet, those
same walls inspired one man so much that he commissioned a
painting of himself sitting in front of them, and then went on to

inspire millions with his extravagant tales of Border adventure. You simply can not begin to talk about the Border without mentioning Sir Walter Scott. It was Scott who put the Border on the map. It was he who opened it up, who recorded and preserved in his ballads and stories an almost forgotten chapter in British history. Scott is the Border and the Border *is* Scott. And that is why I made my next stop that morning, the lovely old house of Abbotsford, where Scott lived and worked and where he wove so many of his tales of fancy and legend.

The sun was shining when I got there, and the trimmed lawns and clipped shrubs looked almost too neat to be true. The spires reared out of leafy woods, flanked and backed by gentle hills. Even today, the house looks so beautifully formed, so meticulously squared off, that in spite of its size it might almost be a toy. And to Scott that is just what it was. A toy. A toy of such immense proportions that it helped to take over his whole life and eventually to end it, for directly or indirectly, Abbotsford killed him. Into its construction he poured every penny he had, and when his resources ran out and he sank deeper and deeper into debt, he worked himself literally into the grave to pay those debts off.

I stepped through the entrance hall where the walls are adorned with oak panelling from the Auld Kirk of Dunfermline, and into the house itself. Scott was a man with a mania for the past, a man in love with the colour and excitement of the Border. He had a passion for collecting things: suits of armour, weapons, works of art, bits of this and that – curios of every description. Even today, the house is full of them. Relics from the battle of Waterloo, swords from the field of Culloden, medallions from the Old Cross of Edinburgh, a silver urn from Lord Byron, an old Touting horn from Hermitage, a pair of thumbscrews, a Spanish double-barrelled flintlock, Rob Roy's sporran, Napoleon's cloak clasp, Robert Burns's tumbler, a lock of Bonnie Prince Charlie's hair, and on one of the mantelpieces – the reputed skull of Robert the Bruce.

Scott was not a Borderer by birth, he was born in Edinburgh, but he came from a Border family, and it was the Border country he loved and which formed the basis of his fame as a writer.

An unfortunate fellow in some ways. At the age of two, a

fever left him with a permanent limp in his right leg and he never got over it. Every conceivable treatment was tried, but the limp remained stubbornly until the end of his life. As a very young boy at the farmhouse of Sandyknowe, he was wrapped in the skin of a dead sheep and made to lie on the parlour floor in the belief that this would have some remedial effect. It did not of course— but on the other hand, the damaged limb certainly did not prevent him taking part in and excelling at sports when he went to school. And by the time he reached manhood, his lameness was more of an irritation than a real hindrance.

He set himself to read for the Bar in 1789, and it was after the Court of Session had risen for the autumn vacation in 1792 that Scott made one of his first forays into the Border country, exploring the valleys and fortresses on horseback and spending the nights in remote shepherd's cottages. Perhaps it was then that the Border wove its spell over him, for by the time he began paying regular attendance at the Parliament House in Edinburgh, he was already famous among his friends as a storyteller.

January 1802, and *The Minstrelsy of the Scottish Border* met with a tumultous reception. One year later he published *Sir Tristam*, and followed that with *The Lay of the Last Minstrel*. Scott's future and reputation as a writer were secure.

When he bought Abbotsford, it was nothing more than a small house and a barn flanking a filthy pond which had been given the name of 'The Clarty Hole'. Scott set about creating what he originally envisaged as a cottage retreat.

"My present intention is to have only two spare bedrooms with dressing rooms," he wrote, "each of which will have, on a pinch, a couch bed, but I cannot relinquish my Border principle of accommodating all the cousins and 'duniwastles' who will rather sleep on chairs and on the floor and in the hayloft, than be absent when folks are gathered together."

Like an insatiable monster, Abbotsford grew and grew. It became his pride and joy. By 1823, it was totally transformed into a large and gracious country home, with library and museum, and roofs of antique carved oak. Scott would wander through its endless halls and passageways and dream up his tales of derring-do. But the extravagant renovation of Abbotsford had resulted in serious drain on Scott's finances. By 1825, despite the success of his literary efforts, he realized he was close to bankruptcy. In a desperate effort to keep his head above water, he poured himself into his work.

"I see before me," he wrote in his diary, "a long, tedious and dark path, but it leads to stainless reputation. If I die in harness – as is very likely – I shall die with honour if I achieve my task, and shall have the thanks of all concerned and the approbation of my own conscience."

He did die – his death was inevitable – he worked himself to a standstill. On 21st September 1832, at the age of sixty-one, he sank into a tranquil sleep from which he never awoke.

What Scott did for the Border is difficult to define. Not only did he spotlight its heritage and history, but in a more practical sense he managed to sustain some of the relics of its past. The three abbeys of Melrose, Kelso and Jedburgh, for example, were falling into decay and would have vanished entirely if Scott had not re-kindled the public's interest in their preservation. So although the romance of the Border had existed for centuries, it was Scott who managed to knit it all together, both in the material sense – as with the Abbeys – and in the aesthetic sense, weaving the old legends and stories into a tapestry of excitement, colour and romance.

He loved the Border with an all-consuming passion.

"To my eye," he said, "these grey hills and all this wild border country have beauties peculiar to themselves. I like the very nakedness of the land; it has something bold and stern and solitary about it. When I have been for some time in the rich scenery about Edinburgh – which is like an ornamental garden – I begin to wish myself back again among my own honest grey hills, and if I did not see the heather at least once a year I think I should die."

7

The High Country

It was late afternoon by the time I got back to Carter Bar. The hills rolled out in front of me, bumpety, bumpety, bump, green and brown hills with softly-inviting flanks and gentle folds of shadow. Fleecy clouds hurried westward, scuttling across the sky like puffy white crabs. I pushed on up Arks Edge, leaving the highway behind and entering the wildest section of the entire Border, the Cheviots. Friendly monsters, nearly two thousand feet high, they have a sweep and grace that is soothing to the eye and which carries with it a sense of distance and freedom. Come here in mist or driving snow and they can look frightening enough, but on a fine summer afternoon, with the little valleys bursting with woodland and the sun-touched bracken gleaming like dull gold, they seem the most gentle hills on earth.

A relatively recent range formed during the Ice Age and combining a curious mixture of volcanic rock, glacial deposition and granite, they make up some of the finest walking country in these islands. The air is sweet and fresh, the summits uncluttered, the grassy slopes empty except for occasional hill farms or shepherds' huts. The wind carries the scent of sun-warmed moorgrass, heather and peat. Good country, wild country, but with a subtle gentleness that makes it seem like home.

I swung east, following the line of Hungry Law, making for the ridge which would take me eventually clear across the range to the old gypsy stronghold of Kirk Yetholm. Northward, the land rippled into a network of tight little valleys, and even here the Forestry Commission had left its mark. Right and left, spruce trees marched across the landscape, and beyond them huddled the miniature farmhouses of Upper and Nether Hindhope.

Southward, I could see the flat sheen of Catcleugh Reservoir, rimmed by tall trees. Nestling in the lap of the surrounding hills, it did not look like a reservoir at all, but more like a postcard picture of a Scottish loch, all greens and browns and soft russet reds. Although it blended in well with the landscape, it was man-built, and a mammoth job it must have been in those days. It took nearly twenty years to scoop it out of the ground. Digging began in 1889 and it was not completed until 1906. Among other things, a complete wooden village had to be built for the workmen and their families, plus a narrow-gauge railway to transport men and materials from nearby Woodburn. There is a stained glass window in the little church at Byrness, together with a brass memorial inscribed to the men, women and children who died during the reservoir's construction. The list of names numbers over sixty, although I imagine only a percentage of those actually lost their lives through the course of their work.

I kept on going, making good time, feeling good now, feeling glad to be back in my own hills again, stepping out with a rythmic beat, chomp, chomp, chomp, crump, crump, crump, the wind in my face, the sun on my back and the good Cheviot air in my nostrils.

You will find lizards, snakes, deer, badgers and wild goats on these wind-beaten slopes. Ancient settlements, druid circles, iron age fortresses, Roman encampments, they are all here, untouched, unspoiled, too remote for the amateur excavationists to muck up, too inaccessible for the tourist to litter. They are part of the land, forgotten and ignored, and I hope they stay that way.

By early evening I was high on Ogre Hill with the great sweep of valleys and peaks curling out below me. I drank at a tiny brook. The water looked nasty. Its surface was coated with an oily sheen and it tasted brackish.

From my vantage point, I spotted a lone horseman winding his way around the flank of a distant hill. He moved slowly, horse and rider fused into one. It was a shepherd bringing in his flock. Like everything else in the Cheviots, he seemed timeless, untouched by the seasons or the passing years. He might have been the same shepherd I had seen as a boy on my first trip into the hills, for nothing changes here. Slate roofs instead of thatch, wire fences instead of wood, but basically the hills are unalterable, and sheep farming has been going on along their quiet valleys for hundreds of years. There are more than a million sheep in Northumberland, one for every acre, and most of them spend their lives on the wild Cheviot slopes, for it is good pastureland, a good place for sheep to grow up in. Mind you, they have got to be tough. There is no room for namby-pambys. The Cheviots demand a hardy breed, for in extreme winters farms can be cut off by snowdrifts for weeks on end. The ewes are brought down from the higher slopes for lambing in the spring, but as a rule the lambs are left to survive the weather as best they can. Occasionally, some of them are packed off to lower ground to begin with, but thereafter are expected to remain with the rest of the flock.

I think there is nothing more pitiful than the sight of lambs who have survived the winter but whose mothers have died giving them birth. I am afraid I could never be a sheep farmer. I just do not have the stomach for it. I once spent several weeks at a hill farm, and in the field opposite were two orphaned lambs who had been nursed through the early weeks of their life by the farmer's daughter, and had then been put back with the others to graze. They were outsiders naturally: the other sheep would have nothing to do with them, but they wandered happily around the field together, and to some extent seemed to have more life and spirit than the lambs who had been reared by their natural mothers. They were inseperable, and since they were used to human beings, they did not run from the shepherd and his dog. In fact, they found the dog an enthusiastic playmate, and it was quite a sight to see the three of them rolling in the grass together. One morning however, I heard one of the lambs bleating loudly, and going into the field, found that its companion had died during the night. From that moment on, I found the plight of the surviving lamb heartbreaking. Frightened and bewildered, it cried continually. It tried to attach itself to the rest of the flock, but the other sheep chased it away, and each time danger threatened it ran for protection to the body of its dead companion. Even after the carcass had been buried, the lamb never wandered far from its friend's grave, and when night fell would settle itself on the spot where the corpse had lain. I left the farm soon afterward, but I remember the farmer was amused at my concern for he, quite naturally, saw the animal in simple hard cash terms. I sometimes think though that the severity of the hills has an effect upon the men who live there, making them stoical, and to some degree insensitive. I once came across a ewe with its horns entangled in a wire fence, and after trying for some time to free the animal, went in search of the shepherd. He was a cheerful little man who chatted happily all the way back to the sheep then startled me by forcing the animal's head completely around, freeing it from the fence and snapping its neck into the bargain. I suppose they become hardened to that sort of thing, and a shepherd after all can not allow himself to grow fond of his flock, but the man's callousness shocked me that day.

There are two main varieties of sheep on the Border. There is the hornless white-faced species known as the Cheviot, and the more popular hollow-cheeked type called the Blackface. The Cheviot provides the better fleece, for the Blackface yields a coarse wool that is largely unsuitable for clothing, although it makes an ideal base for carpets and similar textiles. Some farmers cross the ewes with rams of other breeds, either to produce lambs which mature more quickly for the butcher, or simply to maintain a stronger flock.

But sheep can be pretty tough customers. I know they look soft and fluffy and stupid, but they are tough all right: hard cases, every one of them. They can endure incredible cold, for example. Blackfaces have been known to survive weeks under snow. Lambs have been born and have clung to life in the harshest of winters.

Throughout the spring and summer, the ewes are brought down to the farms for shearing and dipping, but once that is over, they are sent wandering again. They can graze happily, not only in the grass-dominated valleys, but also on the heather-clustered summits, and since the hill farms are isolated there is no need to confine stock. An average farm will have between two to three thousand ewes grazing over five or six thousand acres of land, which makes you wonder how on earth the shepherds manage to identify their individual flocks. They do it by a system of brands or ear-marks, but in any event sheep do tend to prefer their home patch and will seldom wander more than a couple of miles or so.

Sheep sales at the nearby towns begin in April and go through to late autumn, and more than a hundred thousand sheep change hands during that period. A good Blackface ram can fetch as much as £1,500, which seems a remarkable figure indeed for such a small animal.

But patterns are slowly changing. Each year brings a new pressure on the hill farmers, for young members of the farming families are moving away from the arduous lifestyle and the sheep holdings are beginning to dwindle. There is no panic yet. It has been happening now for years, and will go on for a long time to come. And after all, who can blame them, these young people? It can be a hard life, farming for profit, and nowhere is it harder than in wild hill country like the Cheviots. It takes a special breed of sheep to survive here, and it takes a special breed of shepherd too.

The sun was dipping fast as I slithered off Brownhart Law to the twin Roman camps of Chew Green. Not much to see at first glance, just a couple of squares carved into the hillside and covered over with a thick matting of grass. The odd thing about these camps is that although built primarily for defence, they lie below the high ground and have no view to the north. A signal station had to be constructed and maintained on the ridge above. The camps were supplied by the old Roman road of Dere Street which runs directly beneath them.

This was one of the most isolated outposts of the Roman Empire, and it makes a strange spot to visit on a breathless summer evening. Its very loneliness makes you think of the past. As I said before, that is always an easy thing to do in the Cheviots for time seldom intrudes. A passing aircraft perhaps, an occasional farm – but in between, huge tracts of empty country which have an air of timelessness about them. The hills were here when the Romans came. They were here when the Romans left. They will still be here when the twentieth century and everyone in it is dead and gone, and chances are they will look much the same then as they do now.

Seven o'clock. I had a good three hours of daylight left, possibly more. But I felt tired after poking about Hermitage and Abbotsford, and besides, I liked the idea of spending the night on an old Roman stamping ground, so I found a level spot down by the river and put up my tent.

I had not done very well. In fact, I had covered even less

ground than yesterday. But the sky was tinged with crimson which was a promising sign for tomorrow, I told myself, and I could always make up time with a good solid sprint.

I took off my boot and examined my big toe anxiously: the nails had already rubbed away the outer layer of skin, and the whole area looked raw and bloody. I plunged my foot into the stream and washed it thoroughly, then stuck an Elastoplast over the injured spot. I hobbled around, trying to keep the toe pointed upwards, for the slightest pressure was extremely painful and I knew it would be another day at least before I could get to a cobbler.

I decided that since I had called such an early halt, I might at least enjoy a reasonable dinner, so I got a fire going and cooked a hash of tinned canneloni, sweetcorn and baked beans, peppered with curry powder and washed down with my last can of beer. By the time I had finished, the sky had turned into a pool of liquid gold. I smoked a small cheroot and watched it with a sense of melancholy. I felt like an intruder. The Roman camp behind me, the hill forts and raiders' paths in front of me had turned the hills into a kind of temple. This was no place for a wanderer in wristwatch and Vibram soles. The moodiness of the Border seems to lie in the very pungency of its placenames. Bloody Bush, High Bleak Hope, Deadwater Fell, Blackman's Law, Outer Golden Pot, Oh Me Edge, Copper Snout, Witch's Crag. No wonder its stories and legends seem endless. And if some of them appear, in this day and age, a little too neat and uniform to be believed, they still give a compelling picture of what life was like in old Northumbria.

For instance, a few miles east of the little town of Rothbury stands a ruined Priory called Brinkburn. You get to it by following a narrow track clearly signposted from the main road. If that signpost did not exist, chances are you would travel the road a thousand times and never suspect that the Priory is there. For the building has been constructed inside the loop of the river, and the bluffs are so high and so wooded that it is impossible to spot any sign of habitation until you are no more than twenty feet away. It is not by accident that the monks chose this spot to build on, for its concealing nature helped them survive numerous attempts by Scottish raiders to flush them out. The Scots knew it was there of course. They tried repeatedly to find it. Time and again, the moss troopers swept up the valley, plundering and burning, but always the Priory, with its gold and silver ornaments, remained intact.

Then one day, after the pillagers had carried out a particularly thorough search, the monks made a fatal mistake. Believing themselves to have escaped yet again, they let out a thanksgiving peal of bells. Unfortunately, the raiders had not retreated far. They heard the bells, followed their sound, and the awful business of death and destruction began.

When the burning and killing were done, the Scots re-joined their main party at a small wooden bridge a few miles downriver. Their leader is reputed to have said: "Well done," and from that moment on the bridge became known as the Well Done Bridge – or as it is called today, Weldon Bridge.

I must confess I have always had doubts about the truth of that tale, but I still think it makes a marvellous story. And just twelve miles away, in the little village of Elsdon, lie the fragments of another marvellous story. Elsdon is one of the most attractive of Border villages. Stone cottages cluster a spacious green where geese and ducklings wander freely in the summer. This was a scene of bull-baiting in years gone by, and on the outskirts of the village are huge grassy mounds which cover the remains of a motte-and-bailey Norman castle. High on a hill to the south stands the rotting framework of Winter's Gibbet, where the body of the last man to be hung in chains in England was displayed to passers-by. It is in Elsdon too that many of the victims of the Battle of Otterburn lie buried. Now of all the battles on the Border, Otterburn is the most celebrated, and yet, surprisingly, no-one seems at all clear about what actually happened. Sir Walter Scott put forward one version, and the various ballads differ according to interpretation. But of them all, this is the one I like best.

It was in August 1388, when the Earl of Douglas, having crossed the Tweed and laid Northumberland to waste, rode, fired with triumph, to the very gates of Newcastle itself and called upon the castle commander, Lord Percy, to come down to fight him in single combat. This single combat idea seemed to crop up all over the Border. People were obsessed with fighting each other hand to hand in front of an audience. Either it was regarded as a legitimate way of proving one's manhood, or they were instinctive exhibitionists. At any rate, you can not help feeling a bit sorry for old Percy. After all, Douglas had just spent the last few days raping, looting and killing. His blood was up. He was in the mood for a barney. Percy on the other hand, might well have been suffering from a hangover, or a headcold, or a row with the wife. In any event, there he was on the battlements, and there was Douglas down below tossing out challenges of single combat in front of everyone in sight. What else could Percy do but grab his spear and get stuck in?

The ballad does not state how long the encounter lasted, but it ended, predictably perhaps, with disaster for Percy when "down before the Scottish spear his lady saw him fall."

The Scots turned tail and ran for the Border, but an English force from Newcastle overtook them on the Otterburn hills on the night of 10th August. In the moonlight, among the knee-deep heather, the battle commenced. The Scots were hopelessly outnumbered. They were not, after all, prepared for a full-scale engagement, yet in spite of the odds, when dawn finally broke, the English army had been routed. The only sour note from the Scottish point of view was that their leader, the Earl of Douglas himself, had been killed in the fighting.

The true details of what happened at Otterburn are still obscure. In some versions Lord Percy was not killed but taken prisoner. In others, the Scots were not running away but were waiting for the enemy to arrive. All that is certain is that a battle of some magnitude did take place in August 1388 and both sides have been singing about it ever since.

Of course that is the Border all over. Legends flow thick and fast up here. And nowhere do you feel that sense of the past, that link with ages gone and almost-forgotten, than in the quiet solitude of the Cheviot Hills.

As it happened, that night turned out to be the most memorable and traumatic of the entire trip. I woke up sometime in the early hours. I remember lying there, peering at the tent roof, filled with that odd sensation that something was wrong. The air smelled different. Mingled with the scent of stretched canvas was a moist humid odour. The temperature had dropped too: I was shivering. I tried to look at my watch, but in the gloom the pointers were invisible. Then, from somewhere very far away I heard a menacing rumble, like a train passing through a distant tunnel. I held my breath and listened. It began low down at first, then it swelled, growing louder, growing stronger, sliding up the entire scale of conceivable sound. I knew what it was. I had heard it before. That frightening awe-inspiring clamour was the wind buffeting its way down the valley like a stampeding army. The weather had changed, as it so frequently does in hill country, and I was about to get it in the neck.

Whoomphety-whoomphety-whoomphety-whoomph, I listened to the tumult thundering towards me. I tensed my limbs and gritted my teeth as, like the hammer of God, it struck. My flimsy tent seemed as if it had been seized by a giant hand, tugging, mauling, twisting. It danced and twitched under the strain. I gulped and bit my lip, waiting for the tortured canvas to be ripped into shreds. I could hear the strained creak of the guy ropes, the squeaking of foldable poles. Aaaaaaaaaah-haaaaaaaaa, the wind shrieked. Wuf-wuf-wuf, the canvas cracked. It heaved and pulled, trying to break free from the pegs which held it to the earth. I heard the storm battering on west like a giant tidal wave and for the next half-minute the air around me was still. I peered into the shadows, waiting for the second salvo. It came at once, a low rumble that swelled into a roar as it ricocheted up the valley. I counted the seconds: One, two, three, then it hit: Powwhampowheeeee, homp, homp, homp. The tent bucked like a wild thing. This time it will go, I thought: It *has* to go. The wind hit it and hit it and hit it. The roof caved in, billowing down to meet my face then whipping just as smartly the other way as the gale switched direction. How long, I wondered could it stand the strain?

Suddenly, lightning flashed, and the sky ripped open in a deafening reverberating explosion as thunder clattered across the hills. My mouth felt dry. It is only a storm, I thought. It will pass, storms always do. But somehow, the inordinate force of the gale and the sharply illuminating flashes which came one upon the other like an artillery barrage, seemed in that time-worn setting to have no end and no beginning. At first, there were distinct pauses between the flashes and the explosions, but as the minutes went by, the time lapse narrowed until at last both thunder and lightning were simultaneous.

The smell of moisture was so strong that the air reeked of it. I could almost taste the electricity which hung, invisible, above my face. Scattered memories of lightning myths flitted through my brain, old wives' tales, fuddy-duddy warnings: do not stand under trees: do not wear anything bright: do not touch metal and do not sit in open fields. What on earth was I going to do, I wondered, if the lightning came streaking across the ridge looking for some handy projection to speed its way into the earth? There was only me in my brave little tent. It would pierce us like shish-kebab. I would be done to a turn, burnt to a cinder. It was a chilling thought and I did not go to sleep again.

When the rain came, it was almost a relief, an end to the waiting. First, there was a patter, very light, on the tent roof, so light in fact that for a moment I mistook the sound for a new strategy of the wind's. Then the patter turned into a deluge and I knew that the heavens had opened. Down it came, with an unbelievable intensity. The wind caught it, whipping it right and left, hurling it against the sides with such force that the water was driven through the tightly-woven canvas, filling the interior with a fine wet spray.

The wind was hitting me now in a continual barrage, sometimes hurtling up the valley to ram me head-on, sometimes sneaking around the back to blast its way in from the rear. I began to see the wind as a living force, intent on my destruction, tugging and pushing, heaving and straining like some tenacious animal trying to get at me in my lair.

Drops of water pattered on my face and I realized the tent poles had become already so saturated that the rain was squeezing in at their tips. I slid my hand along the waterproof suit which served as a groundsheet and touched something wet. A pool had gathered in the shallow basin where my backside lay. Everywhere I reached felt wet. My clothes, bunched under my head felt wet. My sleeping bag, zipped up to my chin felt wet. Water was trickling through the roof, squeezing through the flaps, sliding under the guys. The ground had taken all it could swallow. I was camping virtually on a soggy sponge.

There was nothing else for it but to get out and size up the situation from the outside. I wriggled out of the sleeping bag and pushed my way naked into the rain. The icy spray made me gasp as it touched my skin. The darkness was almost total. I could see only dimly the deluge that came lashing in from all directions, whipped by the wind into a whirling funnel.

The river – or rather, the burn, gleamed whitely in the shadow: it spluttered and gurgled its way over boulders which yesterday had been baked smooth by the sun. The tent pitched and rolled in torment. I started to dig a trench around it, hoping to stop the water sliding beneath its walls but the only tool I had was my knife, and the faster I tore at the peaty turf, the faster it turned into basins of treacly mud. I was chilled to the bone and shivering all over. The wind ripped in again, driving the rain against me in a stinging spray. I gave up and dived for the sanctuary of my sleeping bag. By now, my body was shining like sealskin and I felt a sense of misery so complete that I wished I had never heard of the Border, let alone been so foolish as to attempt to walk it.

God knows how long I lay there, listening to the frenzied flapping of my tiny shelter. I was engulfed in pandemonium. My body felt worn to a frazzle. Wet and shaking, I stared dejectedly into the darkness. Sometime around four the rain slackened, and the wind, although it continued to blow, did so on a more even keel that seemed perhaps less alarming. At any rate, not long after that, either from relief or exhaustion or both, I fell fast asleep.

Morning came with a sun that, even at eight a.m. seemed about to burn a hole in the roof of my tent. It was just too much to accept. I shuffled out naked and peered around. Apart from the swollen river, there was no sign at all of the night's turmoil. The hills looked crystal clear, every creek bed, every blade of grass too sharply-etched to be real, like those autumnal paintings which display such detail you know no human eye could take it in. There was that fresh after-rain smell that gives you a sense of the world renewing itself.

I scrubbed myself thoroughly in the brook, then got the fire going and cooked breakfast. It was not easy. Most of the wood I found was saturated and I finally got the flames started with a handful of dried bracken that had somehow missed the night's deluge. I was in for a hot morning, I could see that, but I had to get my things dried out before I could push on. Besides, I felt lazy. I have got scads of time, I thought, why rush and spoil it all?

My spirits were rising as the sun got stronger. After breakfast, I spread everything out to dry, then lay down in the grass and sunbathed for an hour or two. No-one came. I hardly thought they would. Privacy is one thing you can count on in the Cheviots. They have their moods, those hills. They chew you up like a pack of hungry wolves, they batter you with gales, drench you with rain, rip the stuffing out of you with sleet and fog, but every so often there are moments, like today, when the sun comes out, when the land is caught in a hush of breathless heat and there is a silence so intense that it is almost painful to listen to.

I was recovering rapidly. In the clean sunwarmed air, I began to feel human again. My thigh and calf muscles were hardening up, and even the raw spot on my big toe felt better now that the storm was over.

By eleven o'clock I decided I had thawed enough. It was time to move. I took down my tent, which had dried out completely, packed my haversack and set off along the line of the ridge. That first hundred yards seemed to take a monumental amount of effort. It may have been the heat, or perhaps my body was still suffering from the punishment of the storm, but for almost an hour I felt like a man who had just come out of a coma. Nothing seemed to work right. My knees, my ankles, even my elbows felt disjointed. Worse still, I was puffing like a steamroller, huffing and hissing, sucking and gasping, my lungs going fifteen to the dozen like overworked football bladders.

Things grew better after a while. I got my second wind and swung into that semi-automatic lope that carries on by reflex almost, for hour after hour.

The land here seemed divided into two parts. On my left, sweeping away to the Scottish lowlands, valleys and rivers intertwined in an intricate framework of green and brown, orange and gold. There were tiny farms down there, telescopic blobs of white which clung to strips of woodland or patchwork fields carved out of the primitive peat. On my right, the land rippled south, wild and hard and unyielding.

Sweat ran down my face. I stopped to take off my shirt and tuck it under my haversack flap. It didn't help much, for within seconds my skin was glistening as if it had been rubbed with oil. Thirst pangs were troubling me too, and whenever I crossed a river I stopped to kneel and drink. Trouble was, the more I swallowed the more I wanted, until in the end I decided the only way to fight it was to ignore my thirst completely.

On and on, up and up, left foot, right foot, I just kept going, tappety-tappety-bumpety-bump.

I paused for breath and spotted on the tip of a distant hill, a solitary whitewashed notice board. It made an incongruous sight, perched all alone in the heather, and curiosity aroused, I felt I had to investigate, even though it meant wandering from my path.

It took me thirty minutes to get there for the damn thing was facing the other way and I couldn't read what it said until I was actually standing beside it. The words gave me a momentary chill.

DANGER – UNCLEARED MILITARY TARGET AREA
DO NOT TOUCH ANYTHING – IT MAY EXPLODE AND
KILL YOU

I peered frantically around for something not to touch. I was desperately willing not to touch anything at all, but the grass was knee-deep, so if there was anything I shouldn't be touching, I obviously would not be aware of it until I already had.

At that moment, I noticed the nearby angry crackle of artillery fire and realized I had wandered into the area I was looking for, the army firing range.

Nearly 60,000 acres of moorland and hill country between the River Rede and the Scottish Border make up one of the major military training areas in Great Britain. During the course of each year, something like 300 units come to train here, generally for periods of a week or a fortnight at a time and every type of firing is practised, from the heaviest artillery down to air-to-ground missiles and even sub-machine guns. The only type of weapon which cannot manoeuvre in the soft clinging peat thank God, is the battle tank. I shudder to think of the mess those great caterpillar treads could make of the beautiful grassy hillsides. (I learned later that some of the heaviest guns fire over the main Newcastle–Jedburgh road, which struck me as an alarming thought. I was assured happily by the cheery colonel in command that there had not been a mistake yet.)

Red flags fly around the range boundaries when firing is in progress, except for one month each year, from mid-April to mid-May, when all training stops to allow the farmers to get on with their lambing, for the land has been divided into thirty hill farms which are leased out by the Ministry of Defence to civilian farmers. 30,000 sheep and 1,500 cattle graze under the muzzles of the big guns.

But the real purpose of the army land is its military role. The range is divided into two parts by the upper reaches of the river Coquet. The northern section, which lies between the river and the Border is known as the Dry Training Area. This is steep hill country rising up to 2,000 feet above sea level, and generally speaking is unfit for wheeled vehicles, even landrovers. No actual firing is carried out here. It is used instead for specialized training like mountain warfare, 'cordon and search', 'escape and evasion', and various types of endurance test. It was this section I was due to penetrate later that afternoon, but first I wanted to pay a visit to the base of operations, the hutted camp near Otterburn where the army H.Q. is located.

I do not know what I expected: precision, uniforms, armed guards, that kind of thing, I suppose. As it happened, nobody stopped me, and the only uniform I saw was a Naafi overall on a lady emptying rubbish into a dustbin.

Sheep roamed happily over the patches of neatly-trimmed grass, and nestling among the cluster of military huts stood a stone-built traditional Northumbrian farmhouse.

I found the H.Q. easily enough, and was ushered in to meet the commanding officer, Lieutenant Colonel John Stephenson. I liked him at once. He was a handsome suntanned man in his early fifties who seemed happy to talk about his work, and the function of the range he controlled. I asked him if he was not worried about the apparent lack of security. He smiled.

"What's the point?" he said, "There's nothing to guard against. The units which come here to train bring their own equipment with them. If there was an important exercise going on, you would find security tight enough, but at the moment the range is practically empty."

As it happened, the film crew had arrived before me, and now they came trotting in from the office next door, clutching mugs of strong black coffee. I sensed from the tight little smiles on their faces that something was up.

"We've got a surprise for you," announced Matthew, my director.

"Oh?" I said cautiously.

"We want you to take on the S.A.S."

I stared at him blankly. The S.A.S. I had heard of the S.A.S. – the Special Air Services – top secret branch of the British army. Let's face it, who hasn't?

The S.A.S. are the army's secret agents. They were founded by Colonel David Stirling in North Africa in 1941 for the purpose of carrying out raids on targets far behind enemy lines. They were used for jungle operations in Malaya during the troubles of the 1950s, and later in Oman, Indonesia and Borneo, and against the rebels in Aden. That is all anyone seems to know about them. Reporters refer to them as the James Bond soldiers because their degree of secrecy is so intense that even the highest-ranking officers of the British army know them only as strange silent men who arrive, often in the dead of night, in uniforms which carry no insignia of any kind, and who refuse to identify themselves, or to discuss their ranks, skills or operations.

But that was not all. I knew they were reputed to be tough, tenacious, and when the occasion demanded it, utterly ruthless. Their motto is "Who Dares Wins", and every member of the S.A.S. is adept at parachuting, sabotage, unarmed combat and mountain warfare. The selection course is said to be so strenuous that only a handful of volunteers manage to see it through. They are a rough mob, and no mistake.

I looked from face to face. They stared back impassively.

"Would you repeat that?" I whispered softly.

"We want you to take on the S.A.S.," proclaimed Matthew for the second time.

"That's what I thought you said."

I looked at the Colonel.

"The S.A.S. are training *here*?" I asked.

He nodded.

"A bunch of them are. They're using the Dry Training Area for some exercise or other. They're not usually very happy about welcoming visitors."

I turned back to Matthew.

"What do you mean by 'take them on'?" I demanded.

He shrugged lightly.

"We thought you might wander in without tipping them off, and see what happens," he said.

"You must be out of your mind."

"It's quite safe really. I mean, they won't shoot you dead or anything like that. They're in the Dry Training Area, and there's no live ammunition allowed."

"That's a comfort," I said frostily, "they'll have to club me to death."

I turned to the Colonel.

"What do you think?"

He shrugged.

"I wouldn't recommend it myself," he said, "but it's up to you. I've tipped off the officers, so it's only the men who won't know who you are and what you're up to. You might come out of it all right."

Matthew began to grin. He was lean, slim-hipped and asthetic. When he grinned his face looked uncomfortably insane. I felt the walls closing in around me.

"We'll make a hero out of you," he promised, "It'll be the one bit of film everyone will remember."

The Colonel pushed a pad of paper and pencil across the desk.

"What's that for?" I asked.

"The name and address of your next of kin," he said dryly.

8

Virgin Soldiers

Before confronting the S.A.S., we had another job to do. Aerial shots, by helicopter. The heliport was a small concrete square, cordoned off by high wire fences. I strapped myself into the passenger seat, the cameraman settled into his harness, the pilot gave thumbs-up, and with a great thunder of sound the propellors began their rotation.

The machine shivered and clattered alarmingly, while the pilot checked each of his instruments in turn. Then, with what seemed no warning at all, we were floating upwards into the air with the whole army encampment dwindling away below. There is no sensation that gives you a sense of flight, of being airborn, quite so acutely as that of sitting in a helicopter, particularly one with a transparent nose and deck. Apart from the shudder of the blades, and the constriction of being tighly strapped in, you feel as if you are encased in a bubble floating over the earth. The pilot can, if he chooses, stand still, hover, go up or down, right or left, backwards or forwards. And the beauty of it is, you are still close enough to ground for the contours to mean something: hills are still hills, valleys are still valleys, they have not been wiped out by distance and altitude.

I felt I had never seen anything so beautiful as the moment we launched ourselves into the sky that dazzling lunchtime. The hills seemed to dance beneath us. Grazing sheep clustered the moorgrass like bits of scattered confetti. A network of narrow roads sliced east and west, and I spotted a handful of dummy tanks, their turrets shattered by shrapnel and shellfire. The range looked so peaceful, the hills dipping and swelling beneath us in a great extravagant splash of colour: it was hard to believe they could be used for such a discordant pastime as warfare.

The pilot turned and gestured earthward. I peered down. We were crossing a wide grassy plain, like a huge waterlogged saucer, which would at one time have made a pleasing contrast to the wild fells which surrounded it. Now however, the heather and peat were pockmarked by dozens of shell craters, as if the whole of the earth's surface had erupted in some dreadful skin disease. This was the target area. We glided lower, skimming over the shell holes which lay scattered below us like open sores. There were no sheep here. There was no sign of any life at all. No movement, no colour. A dead man's land, dead, dead, like the surface of the moon. I felt a sense of chill as we floated from cavity to cavity, the cameraman shooting furiously at everything in sight. A ugly place, it seemed. A graveyard. I wanted to be away. I wanted to leave it behind and forget it, this little strip of mangled planet, wipe it out of my mind for ever. The slipshod galaxy of basins flipped below us like a threat. You looked at them and thought of war and destruction, Flanders and Ypres, Hiroshima and Nagasaki. Green and living once. Now a plain of death.

I was glad when we soared away, looped once around the range boundary, and came swaying back into camp, the pilot dropping his machine inch by delicate inch until we were once more settled on the tiny concrete square.

I undid my seatbelt and trotted out, ducking instinctively under the whirling blades. The Colonel was waiting for me by the wire fence. He was smiling.

"Well," he chuckled, "How'd it go?"

"Not bad," I said, "There's a lot of splendid country out there. It's a shame the public never gets to see it."

He looked surprised.

"The public can come in any time firing's not in progress," he said.

I smiled thinly.

"You mean when the red flags aren't flying?"

"Yes."

"They're *always* flying."

"No, no, no, no," he maintained, frowning. "We take them down whenever we can. I know it's not always possible. I mean, if you've finished firing for today but you know that you're likely to begin again tomorrow, there simply isn't time to drive around the entire boundary taking down flags and putting them up again. But anyone who wants to cross the range only needs to phone our H.Q., and we'll say whether it's safe or not. We get lots of calls from rambling clubs and the like, and wherever possible we try to make sure the range is kept open. The last thing we want is to stop people coming into these hills. After all, I'm a bit of a hill man myself."

"Couldn't you put in a system of warning lights?" I asked, "as the Defence Lands Committee suggested in 1973."

He shook his head.

"Not a chance," he said, "It would cost too much for one thing. And then, who's to know if one of the lights isn't working? I'm a lot happier with the system the way it is. If you want to cross the range, give us a ring and we'll keep you right."

I mentioned the warning sign I'd spotted with its ominous warning: "Do not touch anything. It may explode and kill you."

He began to laugh.

"Hardly likely," he admitted, "Most of the unexploded shells were cleared out long ago, and if you were unlucky enough to stumble across one, it wouldn't do you any harm. The only danger is if someone decides to tinker around with a live missile, or to take it home as a souvenir. That's why the warning notices are there. Better to be safe than sorry."

We began to stroll back towards the H.Q.

"What do you think of this S.A.S. idea?" I asked.

"Well, I contacted the officer by radio," he said, "and he seemed to think you were out of your minds, but he's willing to give it a try. He hasn't tipped his men off. Seems he'd like to watch their reaction just as much as you would. My driver will take you up there. It's not far, but it'd take you hours by foot."

I thanked him for his trouble, we shook hands, and I watched him stride back to his office, brisk, efficient, full of life. I liked him. He was frank and direct and he had a sense of fun. I never saw him again. Some months later, he was shot dead by gunmen in the doorway of his Otterburn home.

Our driver, it turned out, thought we were even madder than the Colonel did, and as we bounced and jostled along the rough

dirt road I began to have a few doubts about our sanity myself.
The S.A.S., after all, were trained to kill. To expect no quarter
and to give none either. What were we trying to prove? It
seemed crazy to me, and the idea grew steadily crazier as we
rattled deeper and deeper into the now menacing network of
steep-sided little valleys. Hills crowded in tight and close. Amber
streams swirled down slopes of heather and gorse. Sparkling
burns trickled through beechwood and bilberry. Sheep grazed
through bents and fescues, sweet vernal grass and woodrush.
Such a peaceful scene. What a crime to spoil it. Chug, chug,
chug, we rattled on. The driver whistled a cheerful tune. He had
the amiable contented air of a farmer taking a truckload of lambs
to the abattoir. Behind me, Matthew was tapping his feet in time
to the music. Was I the only one with sanity intact?

Trees filtered down the hillsides, or clung like spirals of soft
green smoke to small jagged outcrops of rock. Great screes
tumbled down to the river like the folds of immense bridal veils.
The hilltops were getting higher, we went on penetrating: one
mile, two miles, how much further? We swung around a bend
and the driver said: "There they are."

I could not see them at first. They were so far away their
combat jackets blended into the hillsides. I half-closed my eyes
and the world swam into focus. There was a flicker of
movement, one here, one there. He was right.

The driver slithered to a halt and turned to us with a grin.

"Try not to hurt them too much," he said.

We glowered at him and began to unload the equipment. It
took about ten minutes, and by the end of that time we were
huffing and puffing like a bunch of old hens. I peered at the crew
in dismay. We were hardly what you could call in fighting trim.

"Are you sure you want to go through with this?" I muttered
to Matthew.

His eyes gleamed with a fanatical fire.

"It'll be the best bit of film we've ever shot," he declared
enthusiastically.

"It might be the last," I grunted, "What now?"

He peered at the slope of the nearest hill. It climbed, almost
perpendicular, for about a thousand feet or more, before easing
off into a conical summit.

"Up there," he announced.

I looked at the hill. I looked at the crew.

"Us?" I murmured in disbelief.

He nodded furiously. We shouldered the gear and began to clamber up the perilous grass-covered incline. It was like trying to walk through a cake of fudge. The equipment creaked against our spines, hauling us back, as inch by inch, foot by foot, we floundered stubbornly upward. I could see the sky, slanting high above my head, and the little rounded tip which I took to be the summit, but which kept receding in a maddeningly tantalizing way the nearer we got to it. It was a hill without end, a monstrous tilting declivity which stretched on to eternity itself. We were gasping, sucking in air like fish out of water, while down below our driver lit himself a cigarette and watched our progress with the wry amusement of a football scout at an old men's bowling tournament.

For the next twenty minutes we were completely out of sight of the soldiers in the valley, which was just as well. If they had discovered us at that point, we would have collapsed like helpless children for it was a gruelling climb, a spine-cracking climb. Camera gear is not built to be hauled up gradients of less than one in two, and we were none of us great white hopes for the summer Olympics. But somehow, either by luck or by a sheer old-fashioned miracle, we got to the top and sprawled in the grass, chests heaving, eyes bulging, puffing, panting, drained and drooping.

By now we were among the topmost summits, and all around us hilltops nudged into the sky like a vast school of surfacing whales. Our own peak joined on to a long smooth ridge that curled along the valley, following the line of the river below.

Someone said: "Where's Bill?"

We looked around.

"Bill?"

Bill was our sound recordist. We found him thirty feet below, clinging to the grass clumps like grim death, his lips peeled back in a desperate grimace, his cheeks glistening like purple grapes. We hauled him up and undid his collar. He sprawled like a landed trout, taking huge bites at the air.

I looked at Matthew.

"Do you think maybe we're a bit outmatched?" I said, giving it one last try.

But Matthew was not having any.

"Let's set the gear up," he ordered, "and get this show on the road."

We played it out as long as we could, sorting out fresh magazines, lacing the film with meticulous time-consuming care, adjusting the straps of the camera harness and testing the gun mike for quality, but in the end the awful moment arrived when we were all set and ready to go.

"Forward," cried Matthew like a crazed dictator, and obediently we moved off along the line of the ridge, following the slender ribbon of river far below. I looked at my watch. It had taken nearly an hour to reach the hilltop and sort ourselves out. "Maybe they won't be there any more," I thought suddenly. The possibility cheered me. I felt better now that we had gained height. Being high gave us back our confidence. We felt superior, immune, too remote to be threatened by danger from below. What fools we were.

The valley suddenly twisted west, and there below us, tinkering around the girders of a tiny Bailey bridge, crouched our S.A.S. men. They looked like toy soldiers, harmless bits of paint and lead, their bodies swathed in berets and camoflaged jackets. Were *they* what we had been afraid of? They might have been a cluster of ants. Insect troops in insect uniforms. How could they harm us, how could they *reach* us? So safe we felt on our mountain refuge.

"Okay," grunted Matthew, "Mark it."

"Slate twenty-four, take one," snapped the camera assistant crisply, and the filming began.

It took the soldiers precisely thirty seconds to spot us: I counted. Thirty seconds, that's all, and we must have been a mile away. One minute they were crouched like bits of motionless fluff beside the bridge, the next they were buzzing furiously about, and we had the uncomfortable sensation of being scrutinized through field glasses.

"They've seen us," I said.

Matthew nodded.

"Now the fun starts."

He nodded again. Did I detect the first glimmer of uncertainty in those bright fanatic eyes? That's all I need, I thought.

Far below, the little group of soldiers fanned out, splitting into two squads, one coming straight up the hillside toward us, the other filtering along the valley floor, presumably to shut off our escape from the rear.

It was the wierdest sensation to stand there and watch them come. They looked so small, so neat and distinct: it was hard to picture them in menacing terms. It might have been a scene from an adventure film. Except that this was a real manhunt and we were the quarry. All sorts of myths about the S.A.S. began flitting through my mind. Their ruthlessness, their tenacity, their legendary determination never to quit, to tackle any job, no matter how dangerous, or how dirty.

"We're in for it now," I said.

Matthew did not answer. We stood like fools, filming away, as bit by bit they inched steadily closer. I could see them clearly now. They were growing larger, taking shape, developing lines and contours and features. They looked tough, fit and sure of themselves, and they kept on coming, never slacking, on and on like mechanical robots which could not be stopped.

"All right," said Matthew, "Let's give them a run for their money."

Feeling like idiots, we gathered the camera equipment together and began to slope off back across the ridge, hobbling along like a bunch of pensioners, while down below the troops, seeing us move, dropped their packs and came on at the double, holding their rifles chest high.

"My God," somebody mumbled, "They're *running* up there."

We scuttled along, clutching our camera stands and harnesses, rolled-up wires and metal canisters, and behind us, hoarse shouts lifted on the sundrenched air.

"Let's surrender," I said reasonably, "Maybe we can offer them money."

"Where's your spirit?" snapped Matthew, who seemed ready to fight to the last man, "You can't disgrace the BBC."

"No," I said. Which was all I could think of to say.

We topped the ridge and saw at once that we had fallen into a trap. The two squads had caught us in a neat pincer movement and the second group, the one that had slid along the valley bed was already scrambling toward us from the front. They were strung out in a line across the hillside, rifles at the ready, making it impossible for any one of us to filter through and escape.

I looked at Matthew who had turned decidedly pale.

"Think of England," I said helpfully.

"Start rolling," he mumbled to the cameraman.

When in doubt, Matthew filmed.

We stood and waited. No heroics. None of us relished the thought of ending up on the wrong end of a bayonet. The soldiers slithered towards us. I peered anxiously from one to the other, looking for some sign of humanity or compassion. They had the faces of homicidal maniacs.

"Never again," I murmured out of the side of my mouth, "will I let you talk me into anything. Anything."

Matthew dug out his handkerchief.

"Maybe we can parley," he said.

"That's the wrong colour. It's red."

"They'll never notice if we wave it vigorously enough."

"Put it away," I said, "In S.A.S. language, that might mean 'I can fight you and your brother too.' "

The two groups began to encircle us, one from the front, one behind. They came in slowly, rifles high, and in another moment we were prisoners.

It took a while to explain what we were doing there, but happily the officer-in-command was soon on hand, and when they realized it was all a put-up job they seemed highly amused. We were escorted down to the valley floor where they brewed up tea on midget metal stoves which folded up to the size of cigarette packets.

They were tanned and friendly, and like the Colonel and his driver, seemed to regard us as minor lunatics. But finding out anything about them – in fact, finding out anything at all – proved to be tougher than drawing teeth. The officer was very handsome. He looked like a slimmed-down version of the *Man From Uncle*. I asked him where he had acquired his suntan. His eyes hooded conspiratorialy.

"Let's just say it was somewhere in Africa," he breathed,

Hermitage Castle

Hermitage Castle: a lavatory, formerly placed on the outside wall
from where the contents overflowed into the moat

All that is left of the great hall and chambers of Hermitage—the bare shell

South of Carter Bar, looking north towards the Border

Scott's View, one of the favourite haunts of Sir Walter Scott

The rolling Cheviots

The wild path along the border ridge

Smailholm Tower

The Twizel Bridge near Coldstream, where the English army crossed
the Till to trap the Scots at Flodden

Sunset on the Border

The Royal Border Bridge at Berwick

Berwick: Elizabethan ramparts

Berwick: The Old Bridge, built in 1624—prior to 1928, it carried the Great North Road

drawing his brows together to show that the conversation was closed.

I was taken momentarily aback.

"Is it true that the S.A.S. are always the first men into a trouble spot and the last men out?" I asked.

He shrugged.

"Who knows?" he said.

"What were you doing down at that bridge?"

"This and that," he grunted.

The conversation hiccupped along in this disjointed way, getting us precisely nowhere. Did he think his men would really have caught us if we had put our minds to it? Oh yes, he had once trailed a man for twelve days on suspicion of being a spy. Where was that? Again, the conspiratorial wink. Let's just say it was somewhere in Europe. Was the S.A.S. still used in combat in this day and age? Who knows? he said. Well, what on earth did they do in peacetime? This and that, he said.

Why all the secrecy? After all, the country was not at war. He shrugged, his favourite expression: it said everything and said nothing. In an effort to deflect attention from himself he began to admire my wristwatch. I took it off and he examined it enthusiastically.

"Where did you get it?" he asked.

I peered furtively around.

"Let's just say it was somewhere in Wigan," I whispered.

The tea-brewing went on amicably for quite some time until someone realized that the pubs were open. He might have announced that a German Panzer Division had suddenly appeared over the brow of the nearby hill. It had much the same effect.

"Into the jeeps," the officer snapped crisply, "packs inside, bodies on top, let's move."

Everywhere was a blur of bustle and confusion. Soldiers raced around packing up stoves, gathering rifles. We stowed our camera gear into the back of the leading landrover and clambered on to its sides, clinging precariously to the struts. Off we went, dipping and lunging madly along the narrow unpaved roadway. The hills went shuddering by in a dizzy blur, and my teeth chattered with every bounce and tremor. I stared into the flushed grinning faces of the S.A.S. men who were obviously enjoying the ride in spite of the fact that every time we floundered through a stream, water shot up our legs in a chilling spray.

I felt a sense of relief when we finally drove into the little village of Alwinton and screeched to a halt in front of the only pub for miles, the Rose and Thistle.

The bar was crammed with shepherds and farmers in greasy overalls and big rubber boots who were slurping glasses of beer beneath the low oak-beamed ceiling. We called in pints for everyone, and after the exertion of the morning, they seemed to go down with a will of their own. A couple of minutes later we were calling them again. Within half-an-hour we had gone through four pints apiece. I was feeling better. Not having eaten since early morning, the concentration of alcohol went straight to my head. I tried to carry on a sober conversation with two of the troops whom I estimated to be around the forty mark.

"You look a bit on the old side for this sort of thing," I suggested.

"Well, most members of the S.A.S. are in their mid or late-thirties," they said, "The emphasis is on mental toughness as well as physical toughness, and it's been found that older men have a greater sense of self-reliance."

"But why all the secrecy?" I asked, "Don't you think you carry it too far?"

They shrugged.

"It's not that we're trying to make a big deal out of it," they said, "But if we refuse to talk about the things we do, people soon stop asking."

"Where do you normally train?"

"Could be anywhere. We might get a phone call right out of the blue, and before we know it we're parachuting into Germany, or even the Far East. There's rarely any warning."

"That must be a bit tough on your wives."

"Well, they know the situation," they explained, "Sometimes they don't see us for months on end. Maybe they don't even know where we are, because it's classified information: they just have to wait till we turn up again."

I stared at him in surprise.

"That must put an awful strain on the marriage," I murmured. They grinned.

"Lots of wives just can't take it," they said, "That's why so many S.A.S. marriages end up on the rocks. The funny thing is, when it comes to the choice, the bloke always seems to plump for the regiment rather than the woman."

I shook my head in amazement. Another round came in. I was feeling better every minute. We were all very jolly. Faces were flushed. The room was hot. There was an air of cosy conviviality.

The S.A.S. sergeant whipped Matthew's natty little deerstalker hat off his head.

"It's just the job for our regimental mascot," he announced.

The sergeant looked like a cross between Jack Dempsey and John Wayne. Matthew decided to let the matter drop.

The suntanned officer was sitting on a high stool watching everything in that secretive clandestine way. A crooked smile slanted the corners of his mouth. He looked, once again, the spy.

I leaned over, peering swiftly around.

"It is raining in Istanbul," I whispered hoarsely.

He frowned, puzzled. His eyes lost their air of conspiracy.

"The black jackal will hunt tonight on the Orient Express," I hissed in my best Richard Hannay manner. He looked at me as if I had gone mad.

They threw us out at three o'clock. The combined tactics of the most highly-skilled unit in Her Majesty's army were no match for the British licensing laws. We were routed. Put to flight. Sent scurrying into the sunshine with our tails between our legs.

We jogged along in the jeep, singing some obscene song or other, and at the farm of Blindburn they dropped me off and said goodbye. I was sorry to see them go. They were tough and friendly and they seemed to know their job. I liked them all.

The track swayed ahead, mounting the ridge in a series of switchback lines that seemed oddly indistinct, blurring one into the other. The hilltops undulated pleasantly as if I was staring at them from the bottom of a deep deep pool. I thought: to hell with it, unslung my pack, lay down in the sun and promptly fell asleep.

9

Over The Hills and Far Away

Crossing the Cheviots should, by rights, take no longer than a couple of days. A good solid hike could get you across in one, although mind you, you have got to be fit. I had done so much shuffling about one way and another that I felt I was destined to stumble around these hills for ever. Still, after my adventures of the afternoon I decided I was in no fit state to continue my journey, and spent the night in a wooden hut near Beefstand Hill. It is worth keeping a lookout for this hut incidentally, if you are walking the Border, particularly when the weather is bad. It was put up by the Rambler's Association for hikers on the Pennine Way, and there is another one on the Schill, facing the lower slopes of Cheviot, not far from the entrance to the Hen Hole. They are dry and comfortable, and reasonably safe as long as the weather is not *too* fierce. I say this because the first attempt to raise a hut on the Border ridge met with disaster. It was constructed by the army high on Cheviot itself, and I remember looking for it one windy weekend and finding that the building had been literally blown to bits. It was strewn all over the place – a door here, a wall there – and like Humpty-Dumpty, not all the king's men could have put it together again. So if you choose to spend the night under a bit of solid roofing, watch those old Cheviot winds because they can be terrifying when they feel like it.

I woke bright as a button when morning dawned, but one glance from the window showed that the fine weather of the two previous days was deteriorating rapidly. The sky looked menacing and seemed to hang above the summits like a soggy blanket. I gobbled down a cold breakfast, anxious now to be on my way, and after packing my haversack and cleaning the hut floor, I set off along the ridge toward Windy Gyle.

Southward, the hills looked grey and hostile; the wind whipped their grasses east and west till the steep slopes seemed to twitch like the skins of angry beasts. Along the little valleys, the colours changed with the drifting cloud; a splodge of purple here, a rim of hazy blue there, the soft green summits blending into a grey-black swirling sky. Clumps of ancient trees sprouted in the folds and valleys like hair on a human skin. I could see the scars of long-forgotten landmarks — a prehistoric roadway, a time-lost furrow or field-marking: in the grey sombreness of the morning, without the sun to soften their tracings, they stood out like a vivid rash. To tell the truth, I did not mind the bleakness. I felt the hills looked as they were meant to look. In the sunshine of the past two days, the smooth flanks of the Cheviots had seemed a little too green, a little too inviting to be true and the desolation of the landscape actually cheered me as I pushed on through the morning, feeling the sweat run between my shoulder-blades and the last effects of yesterday's drinking session oozing out through the pores of my skin.

I wondered what mysterious project the S.A.S. were up to on this surly morning. In a strange way, they seemed to belong here, for these fells were no stranger to warfare, present or past. I may have left the military training ranges behind but I was moving now through ancient battlegrounds, scenes of long-forgotten conflicts where spear parried spear and sword clattered on shield. They are odd hills in some ways, the Cheviots, for — I know I keep on coming back to this — you really can not get away from their past. They wear it like a glove, conjuring up pictures of jingling armour and hostile hoofs. I thought of Ogilvie's famous poem:

> Last night a wind from Lammermuir
> Came roaring up the glen,
> With the tramp of trooping horses
> And the laugh of reckless men.

I do not know, I would not call myself a particularly fanciful man, but my God, if you could wander through these hills on a bleak day and not be struck by thoughts of their violent youth, you would have to be sadly lacking in imagination.

Windy Gyle is one of the highest points on the entire Border, and 'windy' is the perfect name for it. I have never been there when a gale has not been blowing, and that day was no exception. I stood on Russell's Cairn and peered north and south as the wind ripped into my face with the fury of an express train. Far to the right hung the elongated hump of Cheviot itself, sliced down the middle by the rocky scar of the Hen Hole. Behind, the broad sweep of Bloodybush Edge lay cupped by the Usway Burn. In front, the Bowmont Valley wriggled its way north in a series of shaggy furrows and bracken-clad hillslopes laced and interlaced by a dozen filtering streams.

Russell's Cairn is not a particularly impressive one, apart from its view. The hills are littered with cairns, and most of them look as if they have been tossed together in a very haphazard fashion. But the odd thing about Russell's Cairn is that is poses a mystery. Is it *really* Russell's Cairn, or has the original been lost in the mists of time?

The story behind it dates back to the mid 1500s when the Border was at the height of its turmoil. On 27th July 1585, somewhere near the summit on which I was standing, Sir Thomas Kerr of Ferniehurst, Scotland, and Sir John Forster of England took their seats at a Warden's Court to dispose of complaints and offenders from both sides of the Border. Also present was Forster's son-in-law, Lord Francis Russell, a man against whom Ferniehurst had been nursing a secret grudge, for Russell, it is said, had been intercepting code messages of his.

Like many of the old Border incidents, there is still a good deal of confusion about what actually happened, but it seems that an obscure quarrel broke out among the bystanders. Russell rose from the table, went off to sort things out and received a bullet in the chest for his pains. Whether the killing was an accident or cleverly contrived murder is still not known, but it seems likely that Ferniehurst himself was at the bottom of it, for the assassination resulted in his removal from the Wardenship. Some of Russell's soldiers built a cairn on the spot where he died, and if you look at the Ordnance Survey map you will see that the large heap of stones on the summit of Windy Gyle has been named 'Russell's Cairn'. Like the details of the story itself however, this too is in dispute, for the Windy Gyle cairn is of prehistoric construction and probably dates back to the Bronze Age, but it is still referred to in relation to Lord Russell and although it is not one of the more magnificent Border monuments, it is certainly one of the highest.

By noon, I was high on the slopes of Cheviot itself. The Border actually runs around its toes, but I felt I could not pass by without climbing to the top of the highest peak in the range. I was in good company too, for not only Sir Walter Scott but Daniel Defoe wandered over its boggy summit. Defoe's description of his climb is quite amusing. He seems to have allowed his imagination to run riot. You would think from his exaggerations he had been climbing the peak of the Matterhorn at least. And yet, as a hilltop, Cheviot is a mammoth disappointment, for although it rises nearly 3,000 feet above sea level, its height is lost in its sprawling width and length, and it is just about the dullest summit in the whole of the Cheviot range. 300 million years ago, this great hummock was an active volcano on the southern shores of the Devonian land mass: today, it is a morass of mud, peat and wind-scoured granite.

I clambered up the rim of the Hen Hole, a chasm gouged out of the mountain's side like a great open sore, where alpine scurvy grass, chickweed and mossy saxifrage cluster rocky buttresses slicing deep into the very heart of the massif. The Hen Hole is almost certainly glaciated, for the huge rocks have been cracked and shattered by frost action, and peering down into its dark depths I was reminded of Black Adam of Cheviot, the famous freebooter who ravished Fletcher's bride on her wedding day and finally came face to face with the groom himself at the Hen Hole's edge.

> They tottered on the vera brink
> O' that precipice so high;
> Black Adam clung unto a rock,
> For he feared sic death to die.
>
> Slowly right owre then they fell,
> For Fletcher his hold did keep;
> A minute and their twa bodies
> Went crashing doune the steep.
>
> There was a splash as the water flew

Half up the rugged dell;
The torrent rushed and the water gushed
As a' was dethely still."

The chasm began to filter out as I neared the summit, and then there was nothing but row after row of peat furrows where nothing moved and nothing seemed to live. I stumbled on, wondering how on earth a mountain summit could be so wide, until, after a good forty minutes of non-stop scrambling I spotted the white stump of the Ordnance Survey pillar rising out of the mud. There was not much of a view from the pillar that day, and sitting at its foot I began to wonder why I had bothered; it was hardly inspiring, even the climb itself had been nothing more than an hour or so of drudgery. My boots were caked in peat up to the ankle, and I felt as if I had frittered away a couple of hours of good walking time, but after nibbling on a cold bacon sandwich, I drifted a few hundred yards down the eastern flank and caught my first glimpse of the distant North Sea. The Northumberland coast; one of the loneliest and loveliest coastlines in Britain. Even at that distance I could see the tilt of the huge sand dunes at Alnmouth, said to be the site of a heathen temple to the gods Odin and Thor. For this is Norseman country, Viking country, the nearest port of call from the wild fiords which formed their home, and the section of Britain which received the greatest part of their attention. The Vikings certainly made a mess of old Northumbria.

The greatest of all the Norsemen chieftains was Ragnor Lodbrog who spread terror and devastation from the Orkneys all the way to Paris. Ragnor had two wives, both reputed to be extremely beautiful. When the first one, Thora died, he was so stricken with grief that he decided to pour himself whole-heartedly into his life's work, and set off on a non-stop round of rape, theft and murder.

Returning from one of his numerous expeditions, he cast anchor off Spangereid on the Norwegian coast, and despatched some of his men to a small farmhouse for a supply of bread. When they returned they told Ragnor of a young maiden who lived at the farm and whose name was Kraka. There had never been a maiden more lovely, they asserted, not even his former wife Thora. Ragnor was intrigued and sent a message inviting Kraka to come on board, but making this strange stipulation. She was to come neither clad nor unclad, neither fasting nor full, neither alone nor yet in company with any other human creature.

Kraka shook out her long silken hair which reached the entire length of her body, wrapping it around her with a fine net so that she was neither naked nor clothed. She chewed on a piece of leek, tasting food without being fully fed. And taking a dog with her, she went "neither alone nor in company with any human creature". Upon seeing her beauty, Ragnor fell desperately in love and returned from his next voyage to make Kraka his bride.

Kraka seems to have been something of a mystic, for it is said that she tried to prevent him making his final and disastrous attack on the Northumbrian coastline. Her warning turned out to be a prophetic one for Ragnor's ship was caught in a violent storm, and the Vikings, cast ashore, were immediately set upon by a band of Saxons under King Ella, and slain to the last man. Ragnor himself, captured and splattered in blood from a dozen wounds, was hurled into a pit full of poisonous snakes where he was bitten to death.

But that is not the end of the story, for the Norsemen extracted a terrible retribution. The wild chieftains made a solemn oath to avenge the death of their leader and from East Anglia to the tip of Scotland they set the entire coast of Britain alight. Ella, the Saxon king was taken prisoner: the Vikings tore his ribs apart, opening them out and folding them back until his entire chest cage was gaping wide, then they sprinkled the flesh with salt to increase the intensity of his pain. Tynemouth was sacked and burned to the ground. The monasteries of Monkwearmouth and Jarrow were completely destroyed. Throughout Northumbria, the raiders swept in an orgy of death, terror and destruction.

Yes, old Northumberland had its moments all right: the county was a melting pot in those days, not only of peoples but of cultures too. There is a lovely old story attached to the ruins of Dustanburgh Castle, which stands on a rocky promontory between Craster and Embleton, just down the coast from Alnmouth. There are no roads to Dustanburgh: to get there you have to leave your car and walk. It is worth the trip though, not so much for the ruins themselves which are falling to bits, but for the moody atmosphere of the gaunt walls crouching above the foaming breakers of the North Sea.

> And then they cross'd themselves to hear
> The whitening breakers sound so near,
> Where, howling through the rocks they roar
> On Dustanborough's cavern'd shore.

According to legend, a certain gentleman called Sir Guy the Seeker took shelter among the ruins one wild stormy night. While stumbling around inside, he came upon a remarkable scene. In a great hall, lit supernaturally by hidden torches, lay a hundred black marble stallions with a hundred marble knights sleeping on the ground beside them. In the centre, entombed in a block of solid crystal lay a beautiful sleeping maiden. Nearby, on a portal, hung a sword and trumpet. Sir Guy was obviously no shrinking violet for he picked up the trumpet and gave a long loud blast, whereupon the marble stallions began to neigh and paw the ground, the knights leapt suddenly into life, and Sir Guy, his nerve shattered at last, charged headlong out into the angry night. They say he pottered around the ruins for years afterwards looking for the secret chamber which he never again found, and in the end, old and feeble, he went completely out of his mind.

But there is another story from the Northumbrian coast which has nothing to do with the supernatural: it is, in fact, absolutely true. On the rocky outcrops of the Farne Islands, a few miles east of Dunstanborough, stands the remote slender pinnacle of an ancient tower, the remains of the Langstone lighthouse. It was here in the last century that the keeper lived with his daughter, Grace Darling. It must have been a primitive home for a young girl, for by no stretch of the imagination can the Farnes be described as picture-book islands. Little more than clumps of bare rock, coated here and there with a few tufts of spindly turf, treeless, hill-less and utterly desolate, the islands take the full force of every storm which comes crashing across the North Sea.

On 7th September 1838, at three o'clock in the morning, young Grace woke up to hear cries of human anguish mingling with the roar of the gales outside. Rousing her father, she hurried down to the shoreline and was able to discern through the driving rain and wind-whipped spray, the outline of a shattered ship. It was one of those nights when the sky seemed to wrap itself around the earth. The wind tore at the flimsy bits of island vegetation, and the waves hacked at the rock as if they were ready to wash it away completely.

Together, the old man and the young girl pushed their tiny boat out into the boiling water. Somehow they managed to manoeuvre within touching distance of the wreck itself, and while the old man clambered on to the rock to help the survivors, Grace, alone and unaided, kept the boat afloat in the twisting, churning, billowing current. By what seemed a miracle, nine castaways were rescued, but it was three whole days and nights before the storm had dwindled sufficiently to allow them to be taken from the lighthouse and put ashore on the mainland. Four years later, at the age of 25, Grace died of tuberculosis. Her body now lies in Bamborough churchyard.

It seems an ironic end for a girl of such character: you feel it might almost have been better if she had died in the sea than by coughing her lungs out through the slow and corrosive processes of consumption. A Border heroine who had a happier, if not a more tranquil life, was Grizzel Cochrane, the twenty-year-old daughter of Sir John Cochrane. When her father was sentenced to death in Edinburgh for his part in the Duke of Argyle's rising, Grizzel managed to delay the execution in an ingenious manner. First, she found out where the king's messenger, who was bringing the death warrant from London, would be eating, then, dressing herself as a boy, she booked a room at the same inn. While the messenger was having dinner, she stole the bullets out of his pistols and later that night, just north of the little town of Belford, she held him up and made off with his mail bag. With the death warrant lost, there was nothing else for it but to go through the whole process again, with a new warrant and a new messenger. The delay saved Cochrane's life, for his friends managed to secure his pardon and Grizzel's daring little escapade had succeeded.

Standing on the slopes of Cheviot with the wind smashing into my face, I smelled – or imagined I could smell – the first subtle saltspray hint of the sea. To my right, the rounded hump of

Hedgehope loomed into the sky, topped by its inevitable cairn of boulders, and at my feet, one of the most beautiful valleys in England rippled seaward in a flourish of lush grassland, heather, red bracken and soft green trees. It was here, in the old whitewashed farmhouse at Langleeford that Sir Walter Scott spent the autumn of 1791. In a letter to a friend he wrote: "All the day we shoot, fish, walk and ride; dine and sup upon fish struggling from the stream, and the most delicious heath-fed mutton, barn-door fowls, pies, milk-cheese etc., all in perfection; and so much simplicity resides among these hills, that a pen, which could write at least, was not to be found about the house ... till I shot the crow with whose quill I wrote this epistle."

Going down proved a lot easier than coming up, and I made a detour over the northern flank of Cheviot to visit the Iron Age hill fort on Yeavering Bell. It is a strange mountain this one; at first glance it appeared to be two mountains which have been linked through the annals of time into one. It is twin-peaked, with a gentle decline in the middle, like the cleavage between a pair of female breasts. Around the heights runs a distinct rampart, and one theory suggests that this is the site of a Druid's temple, for 'Bell' is associated with 'Baal', the god of fire, and with the worship of Beltane or Midsummer-Eve. Far more likely however, is the assumption that the ruin is an ancient fortress for the whole of the Cheviot range is scattered with prehistoric forts and settlements. When you look at them, it is difficult to imagine how our ancestors managed to live in such inhospitable quarters, for their very locations (they are inevitably perched on exposed summits) conjure up pictures of days and nights of wind, fog, sleet and rain. Still, they were no doubt a hardier people than we are now, and their primary object was one of defence.

You will find that most of the original fortifications have crumbled away, but often the remains of the outer and inner walls, as well as the defensive ditches are still clearly visible. Clear too on some of the sites are the circles of the early huts. At Hownam Law near Morebattle there are 155 of these, which denotes a very large village indeed. At Greaves Ash, not far from Linhope, there are twenty-seven huts in one group and another thirteen less than a hundred yards away. Excavation revealed some huts with paved floors and a diameter of 25 feet, although the majority of them are considerably smaller. The forts were constructed before, during and after the Roman occupation, but of the people who occupied them, little is known apart from the fact that they must have been a testy lot, wild tribesmen who fought not only with the Romans but also among themselves. In fact, it was their inability to get on together, to unite in any common cause, that made the Roman conquest so successful and so complete.

Coming around the steep bank of Easter Tor I had a stroke of luck. I spotted what seemed at first a small flock of dirty grey sheep, but as I drew closer I realized I was approaching the famous wild goats of the Cheviot; a rare sight indeed, for these goats are almost extinct now, and turn and flee at the first sight or scent of man. I began to circle them, coming in with the wind against me. They grazed happily on, unaware of my presence. I counted twelve, including a number of young ones. Their horns were outlined against the sky, and although at a distance they might easily be taken for sheep, somehow the very scragginess of their frames, and the coarse piebald quality of their coats gave them a wild untamed appearance. The goats are not true natives of the Cheviots, but they have been here for longer than anyone can remember, and were probably, generations ago, domesticated. According to the Northumbrian author and naturalist Henry Tegner, they were once hunted from horseback, but now their numbers are so depleted that one good charge would wipe out the entire species.

I had seen them before, years earlier when, again, I had stumbled upon them by accident. At that time their leader was sporting a massive set of horns: they were so huge that he looked more like an African buffalo than a goat. I was sad to see that he was no longer with them, and had to presume that he had died in the meantime.

I shuffled on and managed to get within twenty feet or so before they spotted me. Up went their heads. I stood quite stiff. For a second or two we poised there like a strange ceramic carved into the hillside. Their eyes glared, their horns quivered with indignation. And then, with a flourish, they were off, scampering and scurrying in a quiver of shaggy grey backsides. I was sorry to see them go. For some reason, it gives me a thrill to see wild creatures in their natural surroundings. It is something you never get over, I suppose, that sudden spine-tingling excitement at the glimpse of a roe deer rummaging in birch scrub, or a red fox basking on a sunny slab. You never feel it in a zoo. I have always found zoos depressing places where the animals look dejected and spiritless. It is up in the high country, the wild country that they take on their real personality, and I have always felt it a privilege to be there and to see them there. I remember with affection early mornings in the Canadian Rockies, gliding out across Pyramid Lake in my canoe to watch the bears swinging in the treetops. They would climb to the very tips of straight young saplings, and then rock from side to side till their black bodies almost touched the ground; they thought this was great sport. I would run into huge herds of elk up there too, or sometimes a bull moose, huge, ugly, unwieldy, and yet strangely graceful too in spite of its massive horn-span. (It would tuck the horns along its flanks to lope off through the trees.) I have never been able to understand people who can go out and shoot wild animals for fun. It seems to me a miserable occupation, senseless and impractical. I am not cranky about it. I do not beat my chest and shout slogans at hunt meetings. It is simply something I can not understand, that is all.

The goats incidentally, are not the only wild animals peculiar to the Cheviot country. Just east of Wooler you will find the famous wild cattle of Chillingham. They are, as a species, entirely unique, and are said to be the last remnants of the prehistoric wild oxen which once roamed Britain. Although they are enclosed in about 400 acres of rough grass and woodland, no attempt has been made to domesticate them or to interfere with their natural way of life. They are rather small, with shaggy white hair, black muzzles and black tipped horns which run from eighteen to twenty-four inches in length. They have a brutal code of conduct for, like other wild species, their behaviour patterns have evolved from the need to reproduce and survive. It is only the leader of the herd who is allowed to service the females, and he must win that privilege by the time-worn means of combat. The strongest and fittest of the bulls enjoys the mating facilities of the herd until the day he grows too old to defend himself and is defeated in battle. If the bull is still alive at the end of the fight, he is banished from the herd until he is prepared to acknowledge the supremacy of the new leader.

It sounds, to say the least, a primitive form of behaviour, but it does have its purpose, for the herd is ensuring that only the strongest blood is passed down from generation to generation. Physical strength seems to be the one thing which really counts among the Cheviot wild cattle. They will not tolerate weakness in any form. The herd's attitude to sickness seems just as barbaric as its attitude to mating. If an animal falls ill, it is forced to leave the others. Should it attempt to stay, it is executed at once.

Man at least is capable of pity and compassion. The wild cattle have no room for such luxuries. Their survival depends on brute force. They cannot accept infirmity. I suppose it is this streak of ruthlessness that has allowed them to endure when all other members of their species have long since been extinct.

The heavy bank of grey cloud was beginning to break up as I pushed my way back to the Borderline. A few rays of watery sunshine filtered through, casting mottled shades of grey and gold across the grassy slopes. I looked at my watch. It was three o'clock. Ahead, the ridge bobbed and dipped in a steadily declining rhythm. Soon, I knew, I would leave the hills completely and descend to the ancient gypsy stronghold of Kirk Yetholm.

10

Among The Raggle Taggle Gypsies O

One of the interesting things about this section of the Border is that the route runs directly in line with Britain's first national footpath, the Pennine Way. The Pennine Way held a special significance for me, because I had walked it twice before – and both times for television. But that had been some time ago – four years at least, I estimated. I was amazed to see how deeply ingrained the path across the hills had become since then.

It is quite a story of human determination, the Pennine Way, for although we accept it now as part of our heritage, it took years of squabbling to establish, and a good deal of the credit must go to one man, Tom Stephenson, one-time Secretary of the Ramblers' Association. It was he who dreamed up the idea of a national right-of-way running clear up the backbone of England. But dreaming it up was one thing, getting it established was another. In those days, going into the hills was not the simple business it is now. Most of the southern reaches of the Pennines were privately owned, and farmers and landowners struggled fanatically to keep the walkers out. It was not only blizzards and fog you had to watch out for: game keepers, particularly the younger ones, had a habit of enforcing the law their own way, and a pleasant day's stroll in the peaks could easily end in a savage brawl. It seems strange that landowners should go to such lengths to keep a few hikers off uncultivated fellside, but the hills housed grouse, and for a few weeks each year the wealthy and the privileged wandered over the heather blasting away at everything in sight: so it was to protect the game that the hill country of Derbyshire and southern Yorkshire was put out of bounds to the walker.

The ramblers soon retaliated. Encouraged by Tom Stephenson, they flooded the hills in immense numbers. Some of them were sent to prison, but still they came. Every weekend mass invasions took place on the moors and fells, and as court case followed court case, the landowners slowly, grudgingly opened up a track from Edale to Bleaklow. In time this was linked to the Bronte Moors, and then gradually extended, until bit by bit, the track slid further and further north. On 24th April 1965, at Malham Tarn House, after nearly thirty years of continual struggle, the Pennine Way was officially opened, and Britain's first national footpath running 250 miles from Edale in Derbyshire to Kirk Yetholm in Scotland was at last established.

As I followed its twisting line that bright windy afternoon, I spotted from time to time the scarlet or blue anoraks of other hikers, but I gave them a wide berth. I tend to be a bit unsociable up in the hills. I am afraid I am not much of a mixer at the best of times, and I am seldom over-enthusiastic about other people out on the fells. However, I did come across one woman who was sitting at the foot of a cairn drinking tea from a vacuum flask top. She must have been in her early sixties: her boots were worn and muddy, and her face baked red by the sun. Her eyes looked intensely blue against the brightness of her skin, and she peered at me with a mischievous twinkle when I said I was surprised to see her there. Her name, she said, was Elizabeth Packington, and she had set out from Edale nearly three weeks ago and was now on the last lap of her journey.

"You've done the whole 250 miles by yourself?" I said, surprised.

She smiled.

"What's so odd about that?"

"Well, it's a fair old pull," I said.

She chuckled.

"Don't look so amazed, I'm no stranger to walking. I used to walk a lot in the Lake District and in Wales when my husband was alive. We always talked about doing the Pennine Way but for some reason we just kept putting it off. I suppose it's one of those things you know is there and will still be there next year, so you say: 'Next summer we'll give it a try'. But next summer comes along and you say the same thing and it goes on like that.

Then last year, my husband died, so in one way I suppose you could call this a sentimental journey."

"But crossing the Cheviots all alone, didn't you find that scary?"

She laughed out loud.

"What on earth for? I'm used to this kind of country. I spent last night in a guest house at Byrness and set out at six o'clock this morning."

I raised my eyebrows.

"That's very good going."

She grinned rogueshly.

"I'm a lot tougher than I look," she said.

I believed her. When I reached the top of the next hill, I looked back and she was still sitting there. She seemed as if she belonged somehow, as if she was part of the stonework of the cairn behind her, a strong and remarkably determined lady.

The final halt on the Pennine Way is the tiny village of Kirk Yetholm, and it was into Kirk Yetholm that I came, as evening fell, to replenish my supplies. There are two villages really, standing side by side – Kirk Yetholm and Town Yetholm. They are attractive enough, but I would have given them a very wide berth a couple of hundred years ago, for this was the famous seat of the gypsy kings and queens, the Faas, the Blyths, the Browns and Gordons. A far-from-hospitable people, they were said to dislike strangers as much as they disliked law-enforcers, and any unwary traveller who wandered into Yetholm by accident in those days got a rude awakening.

The gypsies crop up in Border folklore right through the Middle Ages, but it was in the early part of the eighteenth century, when they were given rights of pasture on the village common that they made their home in Yetholm. It is hard to say where they originally came from. They claimed to be descendants of the caste of central India known as Doms, driven from their homeland by Tamur the Tartar. They made money by carrying coal to Kelso and Jedburgh, by tinkering, and also by smuggling, for smuggling was a common practice on all parts of the frontier, particularly after the Act of Union. They had their own royal family and their own 'palace', and the last of the gypsy queens, Esther Faa Blyth, died as late as 1883. She must have been quite a girl, old Esther. She had dark hypnotic eyes, they say, which could penetrate a man's soul at a glance.

The story of how she gained the throne is a wildly colourful one. Her father was Auld Will Faa, and after his death at Coldstream in 1847, several hundred gypsies mounted on asses followed his corpse to Yetholm churchyard. The next royal member to wear the diadem was Charlie Blythe, but when he died there was no male successor to the throne, and for several months a bitter contest raged between the two rival claimants, Esther and her sister Ellen. Although Esther was the elder, and therefore the more natural successor, it appears that Auld Will Faa had expressed a wish before his death that Ellen should reign as queen. Both the girls were said to be powerfully built, and Ellen herself went under the nickname of Black Bearded Nell, which does not exactly conjure up a picture of frail feminine beauty. But according to ancient Romany law, it was decided that the issue should be resolved in combat, the prize to be the throne of the gypsy kingdom.

On the old village green, surrounded by their subjects, the two girls wrestled for supremacy. At the end of the day, Esther emerged victorious. A crown, designed by the village blacksmith, was placed upon her head and she was proclaimed: "Esther Faa Blythe Rutherford, Queen of all the Gypsies in the Northern Kingdom – challenge who dare."

To celebrate the coronation, a banquet was held in the 'palace', an old thatched cottage which has been restored and which still stands today.

The Romanies had their own language too, according to a fascinating picture of them printed in the New Statistical Account for Roxburgh in 1834. It reads:

… I find that the language spoken by the Kirk Yetholm clans corresponds very nearly with that spoken by the English and Turkish gypsies, and that most of these also have been traced to an Indian origin. On this subject however, they observe a profound secrecy.

Their occupations are various. There are two who manufacture horn into spoons: one tinker and most or all of the rest are 'muggers', or, as they prefer being called, 'potters' or 'travellers', who carry earthenware about the country for sale. These last also frequently employ themselves in making besoms and baskets.

The men occupy themselves in fishing and poaching, in both of which they are generally expert. The children accompany the females or collect decayed wood for fuel. At night the whole family sleep under the tent, the covering of which is generally woollen cloth, and is the same usually that covers their cart during the day. A dog, chained under the cart, protects their property, and at night gives warning of danger. This is their mode of life, even in the coldest and wettest weather of spring, or the beginning of winter. The ground, from which, while they sleep, they are separated only by a blanket or slight mattress laid on some straw, must frequently, of course, be completely saturated with rain: nevertheless, I have never understood that these people are troubled with colds and rheumatisms, to which this mode of life seems almost unavoidably to expose them. Indeed, both at home and abroad, they enjoy the best health. Their quarrel is seldom known but to themselves. I think it deserving of remark, that most of the murders for which gypsies have been condemned seem to have been committed upon persons of their own tribe, in the heat and violence of passion, the consequence of some old family feud, or upon strangers of other clans for invading what they regard as their territory. ...

One of the great heroes of Yetholm was Johnny Faa, hero of the famous ballad, 'Gypsie Laddie'. Since this ballad appears in one form or other in the folklore of practically every country in the world, it seems unlikely that it actually originated in Yetholm, but this version is still sung in the Borderlands. It tells how Faa ran off with the beautiful Countess of Cassillis, and when overtaken by the outraged husband, how he and his men were hanged upon the 'Dule' Tree.

> The gypsies they came to my Lord Cassillis' yett,
> And O but they sang bonnie,
> They sang sae sweet and sae complete,
> That down came our fair ladie.
>
> She gave to them the good wheat bread,
> And they gave her the ginger,
> But she gave them a far better thing
> The gold ring off her finger.

Will ye go with me, my hinny and my heart
Will ye go with me, my dearie?
And I will swear by the staff of my spear
That your lord shall nae mair come near ye.

They wandered high and they wandered low,
They wandered late and early,
Until they came to that wan water
And by this time she was wearie.

By and by came home this noble lord
And asking for his ladie,
The one did cry, the other did reply,
'She's gone with the gypsie laddie.'

Go saddle to me the black, he says,
The brown rides never so speedie,
And I will neither eat nor drink
Till I bring home my ladie.

He wandered high, he wandered low,
He wandered late and early,
Until he came to that wan water
And there he spied his ladie.

O wilt thou come home, my hinny and my heart,
O wilt thou come home my dearie?
And I'll keep thee in a close room,
Where no man shall come near thee.

I will not go home, my hinny and my heart,
I will not go home my dearie,
If I have breun good beer, I'll drink of the same,
And my Lord shall nae mau'r come near me.

But they were fifteen valiant men,
Black, but very bonnie,
And they lost all their lives for one,
The Earl of Cassillis' ladie.

Another famous Yetholm character was Jean Gordon, said to
the original of Scott's Meg Merrilees. She was born in the village

toward the end of the seventeenth century, and like Esther Faa Blyth, she too must have been quite a woman. Well over six feet in height, she married a chieftain named Patrick Faa, and when one of her sons, Alexander, was murdered in 1714 by a man called Robert Johnson, Meg tracked him down to the Continent, pursuing him relentlessly from city to city until at last he was captured and hanged at Jedburgh's Gallow Hill.

Jean's sons seem to have been a wild lot. They were constantly in trouble with the law. On one single day, several of them were condemned to be hanged at Jedburgh: the sentence was duly carried out.

In her later years, she wandered the countryside like a tramp, and came to a sticky end in Carlisle. It was just at the fall of the Jacobite rebellion, and the heads of several of the rebel leaders had been stuck on spikes at Scotsgate. Jean was a great champion of the Stuart cause, and began publicly to declare her loyalty to Bonnie Prince Charlie. She was surrounded by a rabble who stoned her, beat her, dragged her to the river and immersed her in the freezing water. It is said that each time she surfaced she yelled defiantly: "Up wi' Charlie yet, up wi' Charlie yet".

They left her alone at last, to crawl under a nearby hedge, and it was here she died in the night, either from exposure or from the treatment she had received at the hands of the crowd. She was a lonely pitiful old woman, but what a life she must have led. Not one of society's pillars perhaps, but a lady of remarkable tenacity and character, and a great raw appetite for living.

I stopped at one of the village shops to buy food and a fresh pack of teabags, then dropped in at the local for a quick pint of beer before pressing on to Kelso. The landlord was a cheery-faced man with an enormous R.A.F. moustache. I asked if he got many hikers from the Pennine Way.

"My God," he laughed, "they swarm in here like locusts in the summer. And you should see the state of some of them. Like walking zombies, they are. And they call it fun."

"What's the fastest anyone's done it?" I asked.

"Well, it takes them three to four weeks on an average. The fitter ones do it in two. But we had a man in here who did the lot, the whole route in four days, in plimsolls, running.

"Good God," I said.

He laughed.

"I suppose you've come to collect your Wainwright's Pint," he said, carefully filling the glass to the brim and setting it down on the counter. I looked blank.

"You've *heard* of Wainwright, haven't you?"

"No," I said, "I've never heard of Wainwright."

"The writer."

"Ah," I said.

"He does travel books. Pencil thin ones, with little pen-and-ink drawings."

"Ah yes," I said, remembering the name at last, "I *have* heard of Wainwright."

"Well, he sends me money from time to time to buy a pint for every hiker who comes into the bar after doing the Pennine Way in one go. Whenever the kitty starts going down, I just drop him a line and he mails me a fresh cheque."

He peered at me suspiciously.

"Where exactly have you come from?" he demanded.

I tried to look as if I was dying of thirst.

"The Solway Firth," I murmured with dignity and hope.

He grunted.

"That'll be twenty-eight pence," he said.

From Yetholm, the frontier line trickles across rolling countryside to the little town of Coldstream. But I was not ready for Coldstream yet. It was Kelso I wanted to see, so I made a detour when I reached the main road and walked back four miles to one of the most charming towns on the Border. Its name comes from the British word 'calch' indicating lime, and the Anglian 'how' meaning an elevated spot. Through time, the name has progressed from Calch-how to Calso and ultimately to Kelso. It is a small town, population four-and-a-half thousand, and it stands at the centre of a very beautiful and prosperous-looking agricultural belt. At one time, Kelso, like the twin Yetholms, was a cluster of two villages, but when the English destroyed the ancient town of Roxburgh across the Tweed, Kelso merged and solidified into the most important settlement in the area. It survived two disastrous fires, in 1645 and 1684, and when the Tweed was eventually straddled Kelso became a town in its own right, overshadowing the ruins of Roxburgh which it had replaced.

There is nothing left of Roxburgh today, but it was once a place of great importance on the Border, and the scene of countless savage battles. Like most of the frontier communities, it changed hands with startling rapidity. One Shrove Tuesday evening, when the village and its castle were in English hands, Sir James Douglas of Scotland ordered his soldiers to cover their armour with black cloaks and to scale the castle walls under the blanket of darkness. A carnival was taking place inside the castle grounds at the time. The Scots gained the parapet using rope ladders, and burst in on the startled guests howling their battlecry, "A Douglas, A Douglas". It may not sound much today but I suppose it sent shivers down English spines in the thirteenth century.

At Roxburgh on another occasion, when the English were again under siege, James II of Scotland was killed by a splinter from a cannon ball. The Queen and her son were in camp at the time, but women must have been made of sturdy stuff in those days, for instead of mourning her husband's death, she reacted by urging the soldiers on to the attack, and the castle garrison was finally overthrown.

The present bridge at Kelso was designed by John Rennie, and is said to have been his pattern for the old Waterloo Bridge in London. I took a stroll along the riverbank, following a neat little path which led by grassy lawns and gracious houses. The Tweed looked sleek and still. Flies hung in soft little clouds above the scarcely rippling water. Bushes clustered the river's edge. The greyness of the early day had faded, and now the air hung heavy with a breathless humidity.

I passed a field filled with donkeys, and began to push my way through webs of tight high grass which cluttered the bank where it curled westward out of sight. I was forced to turn back eventually by a huge stone wall which completely blocked the path. But I consoled myself by walking into the town itself, and visiting the ruins of the ancient abbey. It was founded in 1128 by David 1st, and was said, in its earliest days, to be the wealthiest in all of Scotland. Because of its position however, it suffered continually over three centuries of bloody war, and was finally burned and ruined by the Earl of Hertford in 1545. From then on, what remained of the original structure continued steadily to crumble, for like the Roman wall, it provided an inexpensive source of brick and stone for local builders, and many of the old houses in Kelso are said to have parts of the abbey in their walls.

In 1919, the abbey became the ward of the Ancient Monuments Commission and they prevented it being destroyed completely, but by then, the real damage had already been done, and the only bits left today are the transepts, the choir, the west end and the central tower.

By that evening, I had had enough of roughing it, particularly after my dowsing two nights before. I had now spent six days in the hills, and my clothes were beginning to look as if they had been slept in. I booked in at the Ednam House Hotel which stands on the riverbank just beyond where the Teviot meets the Tweed. The Ednam House is a gracious old mansion fronted by sylvan lawns fringed by dazzling displays of flowers. It is still privately owned, and has none of the impersonality of the large corporate hotels. It is quiet, it is friendly, and the staff actually seemed pleased to see me, although I must have looked a most disreputable visitor.

My room overlooked the river, and there was a bowl of fresh fruit on my dresser top – a nice little touch, to make me feel at home.

I had one thought in mind. Down the corridor I trotted to the bathroom, filled the tub with steaming water and sank into it with a sense of simple ecstasy. Funny how exotic the smallest luxuries can seem when you have been parted from them for a while. I lay soaking myself for nearly an hour till the water at last began to chill and I was obliged to get out and dry myself.

By then it was nearly eight o'clock and I decided to take a pre-dinner stroll around the town itself. It was very still, a beautiful June evening, the air soft and warm. The roofs, pinnacles and little streets looked strangely Continental. Shop windows peeked out through little stone arches. Grey and brown housefronts flanked a wide cobbled square which would have seemed equally at home, I thought, in the Basque country, or in a Pyrennean mountain village.

Back at the hotel, I dined on fresh trout and entrecôte steak, washed down with a good table wine. The waitresses were middle-aged ladies, all Scottish, to whom nothing seemed too much trouble. How civilized it felt. How splendidly elegant and refined to sip my coffee in a pleasant lounge and puff at a fat cigar.

I was filled with a sense of being pampered, of basking in luxury. I felt relaxed, replenished and happily content.

I drank a quick glass of beer in the cocktail bar, then wandered upstairs, wriggled out of my clothes and climbed into bed.

11

The Dark and Bloody Ground

First stop next morning was the little cobbler's shop across the street, where the owner obligingly hammered down the nails in my boot then refused to take payment for it. Marvellous people, the Borderers: a bit withdrawn in some respects, but with a natural kindness and instinctive sense of hospitality that never fails to make you feel welcome.

I was now on the last leg of my journey to the North Sea, but I wanted, before setting out, to visit two notable nearby landmarks. The first was Smailholm, a few miles west of Kelso, without a doubt the finest example of a Pele Tower in the country. I always think one of the strange things about the Border is the fact that you seldom find traditional timber-framed houses with quaint thatched roofs and all the trimmings. But when you think about it, I suppose it is not really strange at all, for as century followed century of strife, anything that could burn was sooner or later set on fire.

The Pele Towers – stern giants of Scottish and Northumbrian architecture – were built out of solid stone, and for that reason have managed to survive the passing years. Some are in ruins, some have been absorbed into twentieth-century houses, but they remain a unique feature of the Border landscape, highlighting the unsettled character of its past and its people. In effect, they were fortified farmsteads, huge stone bastions into which the villagers could flee with their cattle and possessions at the news of approaching raiders. After the battle of Flodden, an Act of 1535 commanded every Scottish Borderer who had land worth more than £100 to build such a tower as a refuge for both himself and his retainers, and of them all, the finest left standing is undoubtedly Smailholm.

I picked up the key at the nearby farmhouse of Sandyknowe, and sauntered up the narrow track which curls to the summit of the steep rocky escarpment. That first glimpse of Smailholm as you round the bend is breathtaking. Here I was in the middle of pleasant fields and rolling farmland, and yet as I came over the outcrop's crest I found myself on a virtual island of wild hill and craggy heath. Cattle roamed around a tiny loch rimmed with water lilies and lichen-crusted boulders. Far below lay the ruins of Dryburgh Abbey, and beyond them, the three peaks of the Eildon Hills. North-west rose the hills of the Gala, Ettrick and Yarrow, and to the south, the distant swell of the Cheviots. Perched on this rocky 700 feet-high escarpment, its gaunt walls silhouetted against the sky, stands the tower itself. It is so charismatic, so steeped in atmosphere that it totally dominates the views which surround it.

Sixty feet high, with walls nine feet thick at the base, Smailholm originally had three or possibly four storeys, linked by a spiral staircase. In accordance with Border tradition, this was built in such a way that should the tower be penetrated and its defenders forced to fight their way upwards floor by floor, their swordarms would be to the outside where the range of movement was freer, whereas the attackers would be obliged to fence against the restrictive proximity of the sandstone wall.

On a massive crag nearby, a beacon fire would be lit to announce the approach of marauders, and it seems likely that a second warning beacon also existed on the tower roof, for two small catwalks still survive on the northern side. One of the duties of a Pele-Tower commander was to light a beacon when under attack so that others in the area would know raiders were about. Mind you, the beacon idea had its drawbacks. People began setting them off at the slightest provocation and there were dozens of false alarms. The teeniest bit of smoke had the countryside in an uproar, but I imagine the inhabitants found that preferable to being caught with their trousers down, and no-one had managed to come up with a better plan for getting the news around in a hurry. The most famous episode occurred in a much later era – the last day of January 1804, in fact, when a farmer set fire to some rubbish on the Lammermuir Hills. A group of nearby watchmen, mistaking his fire for a signal, lit their own beacon in the chill midwinter night, and within an hour, a trail of beacons was crackling merrily clear across the country, and volunteers were flocking in their hundreds to defend the Border, as they thought, against Napoleon and the French army. Confusion reigned all night long. In their bright home-made uniforms, with their rifles and cannon loaded and ready, they gathered in village squares and outside town halls, marching and drilling and setting up barricades, yet dawn broke and not a single Frenchman had been seen. Later in the morning, messengers arrived to tell the would-be combatants that the emergency was over and it was time to go home.

But I imagine those old towers were an enormous comfort to the earlier Borderers. They used them the way we used air raid shelters in World War Two. One whiff of danger and it was everyone behind the ramparts. How secure they must have felt. And to a large extent they were, of course. Once inside, with the gates firmly locked, the defenders were impervious to fire or anything else the raiders cared to hurl at them. Even if the gates got smashed, all they had to do was withdraw to the next floor and use that as a second front. When this happened, the invaders often packed the tower base with peat and set it alight in an attempt to smoke the defenders into submission.

Smailholm was yet another stamping ground of Sir Walter Scott, who was first sent as a young boy to stay at his grandfather's farmhouse at Sandyknowe. It is easy to see the effect the place had on young Scott's imagination when you read his description of the tower in the third Canto of *Marmion*:

> It was a barren scene and wild,
> Where naked cliffs were rudely piled;
> But ever and anon between
> Lay velvet tufts of loveliest green.
> And well the lonely infant knew
> Recesses where the wallflower grew,
> And honeysuckle loved to crawl
> Up the low crag and ruin'd wall.
> I deemed such nooks the sweetest shade
> The sun in all its round surveyed,
> And still I thought that shattered tower
> The mightiest work of human power,

And marvelled as the aged hind
With some strange tale bewitched my mind,
Of foragers who, with headlong force,
Down from that strength had spurr'd their horse,
Their southern rapine to renew,
Far in the distant Cheviots blue;
And home returning fill'd the hall
With revel, wassel-rout, and brawl.
Methought that still with trump and clang,
The gateway's broken arches rang:
Methought grim features, seam'd with scars,
Glared through the window's rusty bars,
And ever, by the winter hearth,
Of tales I heard of woe or mirth,
Of lovers' slights, of ladies' charms,
Of witches' spells, of warriors' arms;
Of patriot battles won of old
By Wallace wight and Bruce the bold;
Of later fields of feud and fight,
When pouring from their Highland height,
The Scottish clans, in headlong sway,
Had swept the scarlet ranks away.

I spent an hour wandering around Smailholm, but in the end I
had to leave, for there was another landmark I wanted to see that
morning. Not as spectacular as the tower perhaps, but far more
significant, and in its own sad way, much more evocative.

It is a bit of a let-down at first glance. A hill, that is all; and not
even a real hill — just a gentle swell in the ground above the
narrow country road that runs by Branxton Church. The slopes
are green and mellow, cluttered with mustard flowers, and on its
tip stands the solitary outline of a little stone cross. How strange
that a battlefield lamented in centuries of legend and song should
today be nothing more than this — a hill with a cross on top. But
it was here in 1513 that Scotland's King James IV caused the
virtual collapse of his nation.

Flodden has been called the saddest monument in Scottish
history. It is also one of the loneliest and least imposing. It has
been called the only battle on English soil that still awakens
sorrow. Well, that may seem a little far-fetched after four and a
half centuries, but it is still remembered certainly, particularly in

the nearby town of Coldstream where they hold memorial services for Flodden every year.

Historians say that Flodden laid the cornerstones of unity, that although there were other battles to follow, it was Flodden which brought about, indirectly, the idea that these two nations might one day be one. It was certainly the last of the great Border battles, though by no means the end of Border devastation and turmoil.

A wind tugged gently at my face and shirt as I climbed the hill. To the north, the Scottish lowlands rolled away, criss-crossed with fields and dotted with gorse and occasional clumps of pine. To the south lay the rippling Northumberland pasturelands rimmed by the grey haze of the Cheviot Hills.

It was another beautiful day. Too beautiful, in fact. You can not think of slaughter and butchery in blazing sunshine, with the birds chirping cheerily under soft summer skies. I felt cheated. I had come to acknowledge the sorrows of the past, but it was not going to be like that.

The cross on the summit was inscribed: "To the brave of both nations".

There was not a soul in sight. Cattle grazed below me. Winding rivers circled sloping meadows. The sun warmed my face, made me lazy, glad to be there, perched on my hill of mustard flowers and uncluttered perspectives. How different, I thought, to that wet and windy September afternoon, when the Scottish forces under James IV tried to fight their way home through the Earl of Surrey's army.

I think the saddest thing of all is that the Battle of Flodden need never have happened. I suppose you could say that about most of the battles in history, but in Scotland the first tentative steps toward unity, or at least affiliation had been taken ten years before, when Princess Margaret, daughter of Henry VII of England was married at Dalkeith to the Scottish king, James. It was a shrewd and deliberate move on the part of Henry, who had already made peace with his ancient enemy France, and who was now casting a speculative eye northward, dreaming of a lasting peace on the Border. It was not going to be an easy job. James was far from a placid king: he was fiery and impatient, and had brought Scotland to the brink of war on more than one occasion. But even he had the sense to see that such a conflict would be a catastrophe for both countries, and that marriage to the Princess Margaret was one way of assuring the support and goodwill of his cousins in the south. It looked for a time as it the age-old differences between Scotland and England would be solved for ever, and although violence along the Border continued in a haphazard way, there were signs that with cordial relations established between London and Edinburgh, even the frontier raiding might presently be stamped out altogether. But then the English king died, and the man who succeeded him, Henry VIII had an altogether different attitude toward Scotland. In the first place, it is obvious that the young Henry did not really take seriously a country so many miles from London. In the second, his entire Scottish policy was one of grasping megalomania, which angered and alienated the very people his father had worked so hard to reconcile.

It was two years later, when Henry joined the Holy League against France that the fat landed squarely in the fire. This placed James of Scotland in a difficult position, for France was a traditional ally of Scotland, and he had no wish to remain friendly with two powers at war with each other. Violence along the Border intensified. At sea, English and Scottish ships began to clash. And finally, the French king made a direct call upon James to demonstrate his support for the French cause by leading a sortie into England. In the late summer of 1513, the Scottish king crossed the line with what was, at that time, the biggest Scottish army ever assembled, nearly one hundred thousand men. They rampaged along the Border, laying waste Norham Castle, Wark Castle, Etal and various other forts and settlements, then turned triumphantly back toward Scotland. They never got there. Standing squarely in their path, with a far inferior army of English soldiers, was Howard, Earl of Surrey. Surrey was one of history's great characters. Largely ignored by his contemporaries, he was a brilliant soldier and a shrewd strategist. Although outnumbered by the Scots, he nevertheless had made a forced march through the appalling weather conditions declaring that he would "make the king of Scotland sorry or die".

On 7th September, he camped at Wooler Haigh Head and sent a message to James to meet him in battle on the plain of Millfield.

James however refused to move. The Scottish king, rich in plunder and drunk with the success of his raid must have been well aware that Surrey's men were not only hopelessly outnumbered, but were also weary and exhausted from their frantic race north.

On the morning of 8th September, Surrey and his army set out toward Berwick as if deciding that discretion was perhaps, after all, the better part of valour. As soon as they were out of sight, they quickly turned west at Barmoor and made camp for the night. Next morning, the astonished Scots watched the English army cross the Till by the Twizel Bridge (which incidentally still stands today, propped up by great timbered struts) and place themselves defiantly between James and the frontier. The Scots now found themselves in a curious position. They were only a matter of miles from their native soil, but they had been neatly and ingeniously cut off. To get home, they would have to fight, and although they greatly outnumbered the opposing force, the very cheekiness of Surrey's manoeuvre must have been disconcerting, to say the least.

James is said to have had some of the finest guns in Europe, and it seems strange that he did not open fire while the English forces were moving into position. It may have been his sense of chivalry, or it may have been ignorance, but when the master of artillery requested permission to bring the guns into action, James refused, saying: "I will have the enemy all in a plain field before me, and essay what they can do".

> The English line stretched east and west,
> and southward were their faces set;
> The Scottish northward proudly prest,
> And manfully their foes they met.

At four o'clock on a dreary wet September afternoon, the battle commenced. Determined not to be outfoxed, the English soldiers took off their footwear and fought in their stockinged feet so that they would not slip on the damp grassy slopes.

Under Huntley and Home, the Scots hurled themselves upon the English right wing commanded by Sir Edward Howard. The English gave way, and for a moment it looked as if the Scots would win through by sheer force of numbers, but while the

Highlanders were wasting their advantage by looting the dead, the main body of the Scottish army was being pushed slowly back, and the Earls of Crawford and Montrose had already been slain. In desperation, the Scots counter-charged, and the English bowmen under Sir Edward Stanley took a heavy toll.

The Scottish army formed a phalanx armed with pikes and spears, the weapons which had proved so deadly against the English cavalry at Bannockburn. Here, however, the situation was reversed, for the English 'bill' with its sharp cutting edge, proved a much more flexible weapon, and in the close-quarter hand-to-hand fighting which followed, the Scottish army was systematically hacked to pieces.

So furiously did James fight, that at one point he almost bore down Surrey's standard, but at the last moment Lord Howard and Sir Edward Stanley came upon him from the east and west flanks. James got down from his horse and fought on foot with sword and shield. The Scots drew themselves into a circle around him, and the last dreadful stages of the battle began. Trapped and encircled, with fresh English forces crowding in at their rear, the Scots struggled stubbornly on.

> By this, though deep the enemy fell,
> Still rose the battle's deadly swell,
> For still the Scots around their King,
> Unbroken, fought in desperate ring.

By nightfall it was all over. The carnage had been done. James himself was dead, the turf was slippery with blood, and what was left of the proud Scottish army lay scattered, wounded and exhausted from the Yetholms to the sea. What a state they must have been in as they turned, with one thought in mind, to get back to their homeland.

> Tweed's echoes heard the ceaseless plash,
> While many a broken band,
> Disorder'd, through the currents dash
> To gain the Scottish land:
> To town and tower, to down and vale,
> To tell red Flodden's dismal tale,
> And raise the universal wail.

According to the history books, there were no reprisals for the Scottish raid. Surrey did not pursue his victory by advancing into Scotland. The chances are that his men were so weary, and the bad weather deteriorating to such an extent that, not wishing to press his luck, he decided to disband his army and make his way southward. Lord Dacre, however, Warden of the English West March who had commanded a troop of border cavalry throughout the battle, took full advantage of the Scottish indisposition to harry and pillage across the frontier, laying waste thirty-three villages in Liddesdale, Ewesdale and Teviotdale.

For the Scots, Flodden was a tragedy from which they never recovered. Ten thousand of their fighting men lay slaughtered, among them all the leading men in the kingdom. There was not a single family of importance in Scotland which did not lose a member in the battle. You only have to look at Jean Elliott's mournful poem to realize the extent of the country's grief:

I've heard the lilting at our ewe-milking
Lasses a-lilting, before the dawn o'day;
But now they are moaning, on ilka green loaning,
The Flowers of the Forest are a' wede away.

At e'en a the gloaming, nae swankies are roaming,
'Bout stacks wi' the lasses at bogle to play;
But ilke ane sits drearie, lamenting her dearie
The Flowers of the Forest are a' wede away.

Dule and awe to the order, sent our lads to the Border,
The English, for ance, by guile won the day;
The Flowers of the Forest, that fought aye the foremost
The prime o' our land, are cauld in the clay.

We hear nae mair lilting at our ewe-milking,
Women and bairns are heartless and wae;
Sighing and moaning on ilka green loaning
The Flowers of the Forest are a' wede away.

"The Flowers of the Forest" — it has quite a ring to it, that phrase. And of all the bagpipe laments, it is certainly the saddest, for the sorrow of a nation found a voice in its strains. Flodden has been called Scotland's greatest tragedy. On one of her monuments there are just these words: "O Flodden Field".

When I got back to the road, I found a large man in tweed slacks and a leather car coat standing in front of a shiny Subaru, watching me in a puzzled way.

"Excuse me," he said with an unmistakable American accent, "I was wondering – uh, do you happen to know where the battle took place around here?"

"Right up there," I told him.

He stared at the hillside in disbelief.

"You mean that's *it*, that's all there is?"

"I'm afraid so."

He turned to a woman who was sitting in the passenger seat of the car.

"You were right, Mo," he said, "This is it okay."

I felt almost sorry for him. He had the air of a man who encountered disappointments all his life. His face was very pale, the cheeks ashen as if he suffered from anaemia. He took out a handkerchief to mop his sweating forehead as he opened the car door for his wife.

"I don't know," he said to me, "This place slays me, you know that? We have been driving around here for one hour and a half. Can you imagine? An hour and a half. We must have gone past it a dozen times. I said to Mo: there must be something, a museum or something. Watch out for a museum, or a restaurant, or at least a road-sign. I mean, you'd think they'd have signs up, right? Is that too much to expect?"

His wife was a tall slender woman with very striking blond hair. When she smiled, her teeth looked too white, too even, as if the accessories of her face were the best that money could buy.

"Our friends all told us we ought to see the Border country," she murmured, "They said it was something very special, y'know? Historic castles and all that. But we have been driving around for a week now and, well ... " She turned to her husband. " ... what's it been like, Harry?"

He shrugged.

"Like stepping back fifty years. You go into a place an' you say: is this the place Walter Scott slept in on such and such a date, and they look at you as if you're nuts? Know what I mean? There are no facilities, no provisions for visitors at all. I'll tell you, this place isn't ready for tourists yet."

"Well," I said, "Some people might find that part of the charm."

He tucked the handkerchief in his top pocket with the flustered movements of a man weighed down by the irritations of life.

"I'm not saying it should be candy floss and hot dogs," he grunted, "But there ought to be a little ... what would you call it? A little *finesse*. Where was that place we went to last Thursday, Mo? The one with the coffee shop out back?"

"Oh, that was where Sir Walter Scott used to live."

"Abbotsford," I said.

"That's it," he nodded. Now somebody's been using his head there. They got souvenir counters and all that dope. They're *geared* to looking after people. But yesterday we went to this battlefield just outside Wooler called Humbleton Hill. Do you know, we took nearly an hour to find that too. There isn't even a sign or a footpath, or *anything*. It's just a hill, that's all."

"And we never did get to walk to the top," his wife echoed with a sense of loss.

He locked his car with the air of a man who expects to have it stolen, but is going through the motions anyway.

"Look at this place," he grunted, "Flodden, one of the most important battles in Scottish history. What does it look like? A turnip field, that's what. It's no use writing up your historic sites in the travel brochures if you don't give people what they want when they get there. You've got to *develop*. I mean, a guy with his head screwed on could really clean up around here, you know that? There's a fortune waiting to be made. What you need is an information centre, a restaurant, a museum, a curio shop or two, that kind of thing. Maybe you could have bagpipe music going out over loudspeakers. I saw that once in a ski resort in Washington state."

He took his wife's arm.

"It was a very important battle, right?" he said, almost accusingly, "You'd think folks were trying to forget it, not remember it."

I looked at the little cross on the hill. It stood outlined against the sky, its grey stone sharply rimmed with gold.

"Oh, I wouldn't say that," I said, "I wouldn't say that at all."

I watched them climb the path, holding on to each other, a very large man and a very slim lady who felt, evidently, that the Border had cheated them. They moved slowly, looking a little lost, a little helpless, as if imbued with the knowledge that when they got to the top, there would be nothing to do.

Not far from Flodden there is a narrow stretch of roadway that is quite extraordinary. The Border runs straight up the middle of it. It is the sort of thing planners try to avoid and it only happens twice along the whole route, but for 300 yards that narrow strip of tarmac and concrete represents the division between Scotland and England.

That may not seem particularly significant in itself, but if you are a motorist unfortunate enough to be picked up by the police on this section, your fate could be a diverse one, depending on which side of the Border you're hauled off to. On breathalyzer charges, Scottish courts tend to fine you about twice as much as English courts. On careless driving charges you can find yourself paying three times more in Scotland. And that is not your only problem. Since they are different laws you can, in theory, end up being charged twice, once in each country – a sobering thought. The moral seems to be, if you are travelling along this particular bit of highway, do not take any chances. Walk.

Flodden is still remembered in the little nearby town of Coldstream. Every year, banner-carrying horsemen parade through the streets, preceded by six scarlet-tunicked Coldstream Guards. Time may have taken the edge off the wounds of the Scots, but it has not dulled their sense of defiance, for the moment the riders reach the Border, half-way over the bridge on the Tweed, they break out of orderly march and canter contemptuously into the country which once defeated them. A memorial service is then conducted by the old stone cross, with the ceremonial laying of wreaths, and a bagpipe lament.

Coldstream itself is a clean pleasant little market town in a delightful setting: it sits overlooking rolling fields which reach all the way to the distant hills.

Like Gretna Green, Coldstream, being on the Border, has had

its share of runaway marriages. Eloping couples used to cross at Smeaton's bridge and make for the old marriage house, recently restored as a tourist attraction. The unofficial 'priests' of Coldstream seem to have been just as colourful as their counterparts at Gretna. There was a certain Mr McEwan, a tailor by trade, who always dressed in a spotless white waistcoat to maintain what he felt to be the dignity of his calling. By contrast there was Patie Mudie who wore a tattered bedraggled suit that looked as if he had been born in it. Then there was Will Dickson, who used to commence his ceremonies with the vital, but hardly lyrical phrase: "What's yer name mon, an' where d'ye come frae?"

The original home of the Coldstream Guards where General Monk assembled the regiment in 1660 stands in the old square, and just north of the high street is The Hirsel, home of Sir Alec Douglas Home.

I left Coldstream with only another fourteen miles to go. Fourteen miles. Nearly there, I thought gleefully. But here the Border, which began by following the line of the river Sark, now ran directly up the middle of the River Tweed. The stream wriggled and looped maddeningly across acre after acre of pastureland, and after doubling back on my tracks several times, as well as making odd detours around private property, I decided in the end to follow the main road which ran parallel to the river, although a few hundred yards distant.

The warm sunshine continued. Too warm. I was drenched in sweat in less than an hour. Walking on the roadway however seemed an undreamed-of luxury after six days of heather and hill country, and it was a quiet road, thankfully. Only the occasional car or truck buzzed by, and I began to enjoy the way it looped and rippled, tracing a path that would lead me eventually to Berwick-upon-Tweed and the coast. Over south, the Cheviots had been all but blotted out by the heat haze. Only their topmost tips were visible, floating aimlessly like distant clouds.

I kept thinking I could smell the sea and peered eagerly ahead each time I topped a rise, but one rise gave way to the next and the fields and farms stretched interminably on.

Rows of swaying wheat dipped away on either side. The grain looked plump and ripe and ready for the picking. Soon, I thought, the combine-harvesters would be going into action and the land would echo to the throb of tractor engines. Curiously enough, one of the earliest mechanical reapers was designed and built on the Border by three Northumbrians: John Common, a Denwick millwright, Henry Ogle, a Newham schoolmaster, and an Alnwick ironfounder called Brown. The year was 1822, and when these men put their new-fangled toy on to the market, expecting approval and acclaim, riots broke out right across the region. Angry farmhands, afraid of losing their livelihood, threatened the lives of the three men who hastily withdrew their invention and went back to their ordinary jobs. For many years it remained in obscurity until eventually Brown emigrated to America. There, he gave the original plans to Cyrus McCormick of Chicago. The Americans had no misgivings about the effects of mechanization on manpower and they swung into production in 1850. John Common was still alive when the first American-built machines began operating in the very fields for which he had designed them – his own Borderland. He must have found it a galling experience.

Morning spread into afternoon. The sun got hotter. The tar bubbles on the highway got bigger. My throat got thicker. At the very next pub, I promised myself, I would stop for a nice cool beer, but mile after mile went by with not a single hostelry in sight.

It was no fun to be hot and thirsty on this endless ribbon of highway, I thought, no fun at all. I was sweltering, melting away. They would find me at nightfall, a splodge of grease on the dusty road.

And then, at last, like the fluttering palms of a desert oasis, I spotted a pub sign less than a half-mile ahead. Saved, I thought triumphantly.

The building looked long and cool. I went inside. Behind the bar, bottles stood in rows of blissful promise. There was no-one about. I jangled my money loudly. Nothing happened. I coughed. No-one came. I rattled on the counter, whistled, shouted, stamped, hammered. I went through to the back and tapped on the doors and windows. All to no avail. The place was like the grave, I thought, I could drain every bottle to its last precious drop and no-one would be any the wiser.

For twenty minutes I stood there and not a soul appeared. In the end I was forced to press on, a decision I came to regret, for it took me more than an hour to reach the next one and by then the damned licensing laws had shut it down.

On I went. Past field and meadow, cottage and farm, following the narrow thread of concrete as it bobbed, twisted and dipped. A sign said six miles to Berwick. Six miles to go. I sang to myself as I jogged along. Bomp, bompety-bompety-bompety-bomp-bomp-bompety-bompety-bomp. It helped a bit, but I could not stand it in the end. I do not sing very well.

Suddenly the road swung out of a wide arc, and far ahead I spotted the distant span of the Royal Border Bridge. I was approaching Berwick-upon-Tweed, centre of one of the most prosperous agricultural districts in northern Britain, and without a doubt the bloodiest town on the Border.

Where The Border Ends

Berwick-upon-Tweed is in some ways a strange town. At first glance, here is a community sitting on the northern bank of a Scottish river – that most Scottish of rivers in fact, the Tweed. It would make the obvious seat for the Scottish county of Berwickshire. Its picturesque houses and latticed windows look Scottish. Its name sounds Scottish. The whole place *feels* Scottish. And yet, astonishingly, Berwick-upon-Tweed is in England.

Oh, the Border follows the river-line all right, but a couple of miles east of the town it suddenly and inexplicably veers northward, curving in an arc to join the coast just below Lamberton and leaving Berwick fairly and squarely on the English side.

The result is a town that is something of an anomaly. For example: although it is English, its football team plays in the Scottish league. It is the headquarters of a Scottish regiment, the Queen's Own Borderers. Its gas supply comes from England, but its electricity from Scotland. Its boy scouts are English, its girl-guides Scottish.

I wandered about asking passers-by what nationality they considered themselves to be. 'English', some said definately. 'Scottish', maintained others. There were one or two who really did not know. One man said, "It depends who I'm drinking with". Another summed it up by saying, "We're not English and we're not Scottish: we're superior to both of them".

And maybe the Berwickers are. For Berwick seems to embody that strange blending of cultural and social differences found only on the Border. In a sense, it capsulates the Border. From the early part of the twelfth century, right through to the middle of the sixteenth century, Berwick changed hands no less than fourteen times. No wonder its inhabitants sometimes ask themselves which country they belong to, for Berwick's history reads like a game of ping-pong: first one side grabbed it, then the other, with disastrous effects, of course, upon the people who lived there.

The town was originally founded by the Saxons, but in those days would almost certainly have played second fiddle to Bamburgh further down the coast, which was a royal city. How times change. Today, Bamburgh is a pleasant little seaside village, distinguished only by its massive castle which has provided various film producers with splendid background scenery.

The first reference to Berwick appears in a charter of Edgar, King of Scotland in 1097, conferring the village on the Bishop of Durham. It did not stay with the English for very long, for from that moment on, it began to switch sides with the sifting fortunes of war. In 1214 it was laid waste by King John, who had its inhabitants brutally tortured and put to death. Berwick again found itself in the firing line in 1296 when 7,000 of its townspeople were slaughtered and the buildings burned to the ground. Strange and gory happenings occurred within its historic walls: the left arm of William Wallace was suspended here in 1305 after he had been hanged and quartered, and one year later, the Countess of Buchan was imprisoned in a cage suspended from the castle walls and exposed to public view, for her participation in the coronation of Robert the Bruce. She was brought down eventually four years later.

Yes, Berwick has had a bloody history, but I was less interested in history that afternoon than in the contents of my stomach – or rather, in the lack of them, for I had not eaten since morning. I dined on a fish and four-pennyworth in one of the town's numerous chippies and, feeling fortified and ready once more for a bit of sightseeing, sauntered out to take a stroll around the city walls.

Berwick has a marvellous set of ramparts, almost intact, and you can walk along their rim for nearly two miles. The sun by this time was hotter than ever, and I began to follow the winding parapets as they looped around narrow wynds and little alleyways, irregular rooftops and mossy tiles. I wondered why no-one had started an artists' colony here. It seemed a perfect setting: as pretty as anything you could find in Cornwall, and without the awful summer invasions.

The first wall around Berwick was begun by Edward I and completed by Edward II. In the beginning there were nineteen towers and five gates in all, plus a retaining wall formed by an earthern embankment behind the main fortification. The oldest section left standing is part of the Elizabethan ramparts which were planned by Sir Richard Lee in 1558 as a defence not only against Scottish attacks, but against expected French attacks too, although these never materialized. They were built largely of earth to begin with, and it was not until later that their present stone facing was attached. The Elizabethan ramparts stand on the landward side of town, facing toward Scotland. They were linked by a masonary wall twenty feet high, and during the seventeenth century the earthworks were raised a further sixteen feet above it.

Peaceful Berwick may be now, but there was a time when the English Government regarded it as the most strategic stronghold in the country, and its pride and joy in those days was Berwick Castle. It is a crying shame about that castle: there is hardly any of it left. It was destroyed, not by vengeful hosts from north of the Border, but by the arrival of the railway just over a century ago. On the spot where the station platform now stands was the Great Hall in which Edward 1st in 1292 was declared in favour of Baliol as King of Scotland. The castle changed hands as many times as Berwick itself, and its history is rugged stuff. Our ancestors were sometimes chivalrous to a fault, but they were treacherous too, and exceptionally brutal. During the siege of Berwick in 1333, when the castle was held by the Scots, the two armies agreed that if the garrison was not relieved by a certain date it would lay down its arms and surrender. According to historian Edmund Bogg, the castle commander was given a safe conduct through the English lines and allowed to ride to the nearby camp of Lord Archibald Douglas for help. In return for this favour, and to secure the agreement, the Scots delivered up the two sons of Berwick's Deputy Governor, Sir Alexander Seton, as hostages.

No sooner were the boys in the English king's hands however, than he demanded the immediate surrender of the town and castle. Seton, who had been left in command, called upon the King, Edward III, not to violate the agreement. Edward replied that if his terms were not complied with within one hour, the boys would be executed in full view of the battlements. When the two Setons were eventually led to the hangman's tree, bound and helpless, their father had to be taken from the parapet by his griefstricken wife.

> They kennt the trad o' their gallant bairns
> As they cam forth to die
> Richard, he mounted the ladder fyrst,
> And threw himself frae the tree.
>
> William, he was his mither's pride,
> And he looked sae bauldy on;
> then kyst his brither's lyefless hand
> When he fand the breath was gone.
>
> He leaped from aff the bitter tree
> And flouchtered in the wynd;
> Twa bonnie flowers to wither thus,
> And a' for yea man's mind!

The place of execution became known by the name of 'Hang A Dyke Neuk'. But that was not the end of the tale. By this time, the Scots, under Lord Archibald Douglas, were riding hard to the rescue. They caught up with the English forces at Halidon Hill and the two armies lined up in battle formation. A huge Scotsman accompanied by a large mastiff strode out between the lines of troops and challenged any English soldier who dared to step forward and meet him in single combat. His challenge was accepted by an English knight called Sir Robert Benhale, a small wiry man of immense strength. While the opposing armies looked on, the two adversaries began to circle each other. The Scotsman released the mastiff which promptly flung itself at Benhale's throat. Being a small man and very light on his feet, Benhale danced nimbly to one side and sliced the dog in two with a single blow of his sword. Benhale's agility, it turned out, won him the day, for he literally ran rings around his opponent, cutting off first one of the Scotsman's arms, then the other, and finally severing his head from his body.

The death blow was like a signal for battle to commence. With a roar of triumph, the English soldiers swarmed in to the attack and the two armies clashed head-on in a desperate conflict which ended that night in disaster for the Scots. Douglas himself was killed, and the place where he fell is still called 'Douglas' Dyke'.

Forty-four years later, the Scots turned the tables when the castle was siezed by fifty Scottish Borderers who held out for eight days against a force of more than ten thousand English. Sadly, the odds proved to be just too great in the end, and when the brave defenders were overrun, the English ruthlessly executed all survivors.

There is little left of the ruins today, apart from the White Wall and a flight of steps which leads to the Water Tower.

But Berwick is more than just a historic museum. It is a place of character and great charm, a popular holiday resort with a busy shopping centre, pleasant parks and gardens, and wide sandy beaches. Its inhabitants number about 12,000 if you include the old town of Berwick on the north bank of the Tweed, and Tweedmouth and Spittal on the south bank.

As I sauntered around the walls, the sun warming my face and chest, I spotted our camera crew filming merrily away in the street below. On the stone parapet, an old man in a grey cloth cap stood watching their antics in sombre silence.

I stood beside him, peering down.

"BBC," he announced in a breathless whisper, anxious to impart what information he had managed to pick up.

"Ah," I said, nodding wisely.

"They're making a film on the Border."

"Ah," I said again. The story of our filming had evidently gone before us. I continued nodding, trying to study the meanderings of the film crew with what seemed a suitable propriety. It was not easy. After all, filming is such a crazy business with clapperboards and re-takes, and everyone getting in everyone's way. My old man seemed far from impressed. He peered at me through narrowed eyes.

"They're waiting for Bob Langley," he announced confidentially.

"Ah," I repeated, as if that was the extent of my vocabulary.

The old man stared at the scene below with undisguised contempt.

"Silly buggers," he grunted, "The Border runs up by Lamberton. He'll never come through here."

I left the walls and walked down to the wide sandy beach to watch the salmon fishermen at work. You can not help feeling sorry for the poor old salmon in Scotland. Everyone is after his blood. Wherever he goes, people are tracking him down, teasing him, tempting him, luring him, enticing him. If only he did not have to come into fresh water to spawn, what a peaceful life he could lead.

A handful of yachts bobbed about in the estuary, their blue and white sails fluttering like bits of coloured tinsel. The sea looked indescribably blue, almost Mediterranean, and little wisps of froth danced where the waves had been caught in the breeze. Beyond the bridges, the town seemed to nose its way through banks of lush green foliage. None of this scenery had any effect upon the fishermen who appeared wholly unimpressed by the beauties of the day. They had a job to do, and that was that. They hauled at their nets, silent, sombre, their faces etched with the unmistakable stamp of boredom and routine.

Salmon fishing has gone on in the Tweed Estuary since the beginnings of time, and in Berwick today it is far more than a sport, it is business, and very big business indeed. All salmon fishing in the rivermouth is controlled by the Berwick Salmon Fisheries Company. At one time, the fish were either sent to Newcastle by land where they were cured then dispatched on to London, or packed in ice and transported south by sea. It was with the opening of the railway that salmon fishing at Berwick really came into its own.

The methods of catching have not changed much over the centuries. The fishermen row their boats in a wide circle, letting out their nets as they go. The net incidentally has a mesh about seven inches round. Once the net has been laid, it is then attached to a winch on the beach and quickly hauled in. I watched them cast three times without catching a solitary fish, but on the fourth cast the net came in crammed with struggling plump salmon, which the fishermen clubbed to death with that oddly detached air. They say fish feel no pain, but this little netful showed all the signs of deep distress as they gasped and wriggled their lives out on the sandy foreshore. I watched sadly as they were tipped into a metal container, and the nets cast out again.

Tweedmouth, on the south bank of the river, was only a tiny

fishing village prior to the start of the last century. For at least
200 years, gypsies and smugglers used the countryside around it
to hide contraband and stolen property. Later, during the early
1880s, the landscape was pockmarked with quarries and pit-
heaps. It was not until around 1860 that the present air of
prosperity began to show itself, when the salmon industry, which
Tweedmouth shares with Berwick, suddenly boomed. Today, it
is not so much a town as a suburb of Berwick itself, but its dock,
built in 1871, is just as busy as ever.

South of Tweedmouth, near Budle Bay, stand the superb crags
called Spindlestone Heughs. It was here that the famous Laidley
Worm is supposed to have lived. The ballad itself dates from the
thirteenth century, and tells how the wicked Queen of
Bamburgh turned her stepdaughter Princess Margaret into a
huge serpent. The serpent is said to have lived in a cave on
Spindlestone Heughs and every night gone slithering around the
countryside, destroying the corn, consuming the crops and
stealing milk from the neighbouring cows. Princess Margaret's
brother, the Childe Wynd, was overseas at the time, but when
news reached him that a terrible monster was laying waste his
homeland, he ordered his men to build a ship, using rowan trees
for the masts as protection against sorcery.

As the Childe Wynd's vessel approached the Northumbrian
coast, the wicked queen sent out her witches to sink it without
trace, but the rowan tree masts proved a perfect shield against the
forces of evil, and the prince and his men reached the beaches in
safety.

When he came face to face with the massive serpent at
Spindlestone Heughs, the Childe Wynd drew his sword and
prepared to do battle, but to his surprise the worm spoke to him
in English, asking him to kiss it three times. Being an enterprising
young man, this he did, and at once the ugly serpent turned into
his sister, the Princess Margaret. The wicked queen got her
desserts when, in keeping with the mood of the tale, she was
turned into a toad.

Beneath the sands of Budle Bay too, is said to lie the ancient
port of Warenmouth. The idea of a sunken community is an
intriguing one, but it seems more likely that it used to stand near
the present-day farm of Newtown. During the thirteenth

century, Warenmouth was the most northerly port in England. It seems to have been a port of some size too, but toward the latter part of the fifteenth century its importance began to deteriorate until finally it disappeared from the map altogether.

The bridges of Berwick are worth a mention. In fact, you can not come to Berwick without being aware of its bridges, particularly the Royal Border Bridge which hangs over the town like a magnificent theatre backcloth. It is one of the finest railway viaducts in the world, and the most spectacular of all the approaches into town is coming along the Tweed with that superb span looming above you. It stands 130 feet above sea level, and its twenty-eight arches – great breathstopping loops which seem to surge to the sky – contain 1,710,000 bricks. It was built in 1850 for what must seem today the remarkably low figure of £153,000.

Before 1928 there were only two bridges over the Tweed at Berwick – the viaduct and the Old Bridge. A beautiful thing, the Old Bridge: built out of weathered red sandstone, it has straddled more than 1,000 feet of the Tweed estuary for over 300 years. This one too has its share of elegant arches, fifteen in all, although they are much smaller than their counterparts on the Border Bridge, for the entire structure is only seventeen to nineteen feet high.

There is a story that one day James VI of Scotland was crossing the Tweed at an old wooden bridge situated about a hundred yards upstream. He was on his way to be crowned James I of Britain, when suddenly the timbers began to tremble to such a degree that the poor king, convinced he was on the threshold of death, hurled himself from his horse and fell to his knees to pray. According to legend, so pleased was he at eventually reaching the other side intact that he resolved there and then to replace the wooden structure with a more secure one. Work was begun in 1610, and fourteen years later the bridge was completed at a cost of £15,000. I suppose it was a remarkable feat of engineering in its day, and it remains remarkable for the volume of traffic that still trundles across it. Prior to the 1920s, it even carried the Great North Road. It was also Berwick's main contact with the south during the era before the building of the railway, when the principle means of passenger transport was by coach. There were several coachlines operating in the mid-eighteenth and nineteenth centuries. There was the Royal Mail Coach, which made its first journey from Newcastle in 1786. There was the Union Coach which opened up in the 1820s, and the Royal William which ran once a day throughout the week at a charge of thirteen shillings if you rode inside, and seven shillings if you rode on top.

In 1928, a third bridge was opened at Berwick — the Royal Tweed Bridge — and this became the principle traffic conveyor. I wish I could say it was as attractive to look at as its two companions. I admit its sheer size and sweep do give it a certain reluctant style, but it looks so misplaced, so hopelessly out of step with the magnificent structures which flank it that you wonder how anyone could have had the bad taste to commission such a design.

I left the bridges eventually and walked out of town, heading north. Evening was coming on and I had just three miles to go. But I was sorry to be leaving, for of all the frontier communities, Berwick seemed the one where the Borderline — that division of two separate countries was most keenly felt. And yet, to the Berwickers themselves, there are not two separate countries at all, but three. As their song says:

> They talk about England and Scotland indeed,
> It's Great Britain, and Ireland, and Berwick-on-Tweed.

The road ran nowhere. Three miles north of Berwick the little tarmac track made a greyish scar through the buttercup-scattered meadows and came to an abrupt halt on a clifftop. A waist-high wall presented a barrier against oblivion. A campsite cluttered the banks of a disused railway siding off to my left. I could see the gaily-coloured tent flaps and hear the shrill laughter of children playing. There was a workmen's hut perched in the grass at the side of the road. A small group of labourers sat in its doorway drinking tea out of big metal mugs.

"Is this the Borderline?" I asked.

They stared at me balefully. Their jaws worked as they chewed at their sandwiches. There was no sign of acknowledgement in their eyes. They might have been looking at a creature from outer space.

"I was wondering if this is where the Scottish Border ends?" I repeated, "There aren't any signs on the road up there."

One of them turned and called through to the back of the hut.

"Hey Jamie, d'ye ken where the Border lies?"

"Aye," said a voice from inside.

There was the sound of leather scraping on wood and a man stepped out. He was big and heavy-shouldered with a beery-red face and ginger hair cropped short military-style.

"The Border, is it?" he asked.

"Yes, please," I said.

"Aye, well ye're a wee bit south. Come away an' I'll show ye."

He put his tea mug on the ground and turned to the others with a word of warning.

"Dinna touch it," he threatened, "or I'll hae yer ears in the morn."

Whether they heard this – or cared – they gave no sign. They went on chewing their sandwiches, watching us both with casual indifference.

I followed Jamie around a field of full-grown wheat and along the side of the main London–Edinburgh railway line. We trudged in single file, the sea on our right, the long coastal cliff meandering off in front, rimmed by clumps of spiky grass.

Jamie turned and peered at my haversack.

"Walking the Border, are ye?" he grunted.

"No," I said, "I've just done it."

"Hae ye now?"

He looked at my boots which were caked in peat, the uppers scraped raw by heather and gorse.

"Aye, I can see ye've come a fair stretch," he said, "Where did ye start frae?"

"The Solway," I said.

"Is tha' a fact."

He grinned suddenly. His teeth were yellow and there was a gap between the two front ones wide enough to stick a cigarette.

"I did a bit o' walking mesel' as a young lad," he announced, "Me an' me father. Up in the Cheviots an' such."

I looked at him with surprise.

"Really?"

"Aye."

"How long ago?" I asked.

"Och, it must have been a good thirty years since, or thereabouts. There were lots of folk wandering the hills in those days. It was right after the war, ye ken, and they were trying to break away frae all the red tape and such like. There was a great movement toward the wide open spaces just after the war."

"Well," I said, "You'd find it a lot emptier now."

"Aye," he smiled, "reckon I would."

We trundled across the next field, picking our way through great clumps of nettles and brambles until we reached the wire fence. The big man stopped, pointed up ahead. The steel track curved around the coast, disappearing into a distant tunnel.

"Ye see that post at the side o' the rail?" he asked.

"Yes," I said.

"Well, that's where the railway crosses from England into Scotland. Turn right there and just follow the fence along to the cliff."

I thanked him and he grinned.

"Nae bother," he said, "It fair takes me back, seeing ye tonight."

He paused.

"Scotsman, are ye?" he asked.

"No," I said, "Northumbrian."

"Ah well," he said sympathetically, "Naebody's perfect. Guid luck to ye, all the same."

I thanked him again and clambered over the wire fence into the meadow.

It turned out to be just as he had said. In a little field, bordered on one side by the railway and on the other by sheer cliffs which dropped sixty feet to the sea, my journey came to an end. It seemed oddly disappointing. I had expected a sign perhaps, a memorial stone. There was nothing. A wire fence, a grassy precipice, the North Sea swirling in shades of purple and coaly grey. This was it. Last stop.

Far out, three steamers chugged their way sedately northward. Evening came crowding in, a soft summer evening that had the breath of sadness in it. Or perhaps the sadness was in me. I had traversed the frontier, following its twisting line a hundred and ten miles from coast to coast. I had reached the end, but instead of being elated, I felt hollowed out inside, incomplete. I sometimes think the human race is geared to look continually at the future, to wait expectantly for Saturday night, and when Saturday night arrives, it is always a bit of a let down.

I peered over the grassy precipice. Sixty feet below, picking its way between the boulders which cluttered the cliff-base stood the remains of an ancient stone wall. So there *was* a monument, after all. Crumbling perhaps, falling to bits perhaps, covered with lichen and tenacious tufts of grass, but a monument nevertheless. It ran from the foot of the cliffs almost to the water's edge as if, in a last act of defiance, someone long ago had decided to make visibly clear that these were two countries, separate and distinct. After all, it took a thousand years to draw that line. It was written in the blood of the people who lived along it. It will take a damn sight more than a thousand years to wipe it out.

I caught a bus back into Berwick and made my way to the railway station. The ticket collector peered at my boots and haversack with wry amusement.

"Giving up?" he asked.

"No," I said, "This is the end of the road."

He looked impressed.

"From where?"

"The Solway."

He winced.

"On foot?"

"Yes."

"I'll stick to trains," he said.

Dusk was falling as I boarded the southbound express. We rumbled across the Royal Border Bridge, Berwick's lights flickering cheerily below. I lit a cheroot and stretched back in the compartment, resting my heels on my haversack top. I was filled with a sense of pleasant indulgence. I was going home.

Index